Your Shoot

Gamekeepering and Management

Your Shoot

Gamekeepering and Management

Ian McCall
of the Game Conservancy

with drawings by Will Garfit

A & C Black · London

First published 1985
by A & C Black (Publishers) Ltd
35 Bedford Row, London WC1R 4JH

Reprinted 1986

British Library Cataloguing in Publication Data

McCall, Ian
   Your shoot: gamekeepering and management.
   1. Game and game-birds – Great Britain
   2. Hunting – Great Britain – Management
   I. Title
   799.2!4   SK311·

ISBN 0-7136-2696-8

ISBN 0-7136-2696-8

Printed in Great Britain
by Anchor Brendon Ltd, Tiptree, Essex

Contents

v

List of Illustrations

Photographs

Drawings and Charts

Acknowledgements

For Kathleen

Most of the information, suggestions, and tips in this book have been passed on to me from others. The Game Conservancy is not only the main game research and advisory organisation in Great Britain, but also the main clearing house for new facts and knowledge on game and shoot management matters and this organisation, its staff, past and present, and the training they have afforded me have given rise to the backbone and much of the flesh of this book.

Two great characters, in particular, require special mention. Nigel Gray for creating and developing the Game Conservancy's advisory service, and Jim Brocklebank, one of the original team of consultants, for taking me under his wing and so tirelessly passing on to me the benefit of his enormous practical knowledge and experience.

Jim was a great gamekeepers' man and to this fraternity of true country characters, I, the Game Conservancy, and this book, owe a great debt. The Game Conservancy and its advisers are constantly seeking to improve the recipes but it is they that do the cooking. Much of the information passed on to me by 'keepers has been vital to the writing of this book but those who have given such help are far too numerous to mention.

I am indebted to Will Garfit for producing the sketches, the front cover and the frontispiece, and to Mike Swan, the Game Convervancy's Technical Information Officer, for drawing the diagrams and silhouettes. The photographic illustrations are a combination of my work supplemented by material taken largely by Nigel Gray, Terence Blank and Charles Coles, and included by kind permission of the Game Conservancy. Hopefully, the book will go a little way to furthering this organisation's objectives of constantly improving game and wildlife conservation and a better quality of shooting.

Finally, my thanks go to Tony Jackson and John Buckland for commissioning the initial series 'Your Shoot Through The Year' for the *Shooting Times* and to all those who, after reading it, suggested that an expanded version in book form must be produced.

Foreword

With an increase in leisure and an associated expansion of interest in the countryside and its activities and pursuits, it is hardly a matter for comment that shooting, and game shooting in particular, has found itself increasingly sought after and popular.

With the decline of the large private shoots, the breaking up of estates and the inevitable emphasis on commercialisation, the syndicate shoot has become the established method of conducting game shooting in Britain today. Of course, the syndicate itself varies enormously from the highly formal and multi-keepered to the do-it-yourself shoot of half-a-dozen close friends clubbing together.

Increasing costs have meant an increase in the number of small, self-keepered shoots and because economies must be made, trial-and-error is not cost effective . . . . but a book of this nature most certainly is!

The substance of *Your Shoot - Gamekeepering and Management* was first published as a series of illustrated articles in *Shooting Times* and *Country Magazine* in 1983. Enlarged and with further information this book, written by a leading exponent of practical shoot management, must be destined to become the handbook for every full and part-time keepered shoot. In fact, keepers of every persuasion are bound to find it of immense value.

Tony Jackson

1 A Shoot of Your Own

The majority of sportsmen and women, whether wild-fowlers, rough shooters or gameshots, participate in shooting primarily for pleasure. Good company, human or perhaps canine, a few testing shots in pleasant surroundings – these are the ingredients for a successful day. The bag should never be of paramount importance. The uncertainty of what will happen next, at any given time or on any given day is very much the major factor giving field sports, and in particular shooting, their excitement and fascination. However, for the host or organiser the enjoyment is often muted by worry unless there is some degree of confidence that a reasonable show can be produced for friends, guests, or syndicate members on the actual days. The greater the knowledge and understanding of shoot management and the more sound the practical gamekeeping, the more certain one can be of the sport that will be produced.

As with all sports, there are many different scales and financial levels at which one can choose to operate. The biggest single item of expenditure on a full-time 'keepered shoot is normally labour, which often comprises between 25% and 50% of the total costs. Therefore, the shooting is likely to be considerably cheaper if the 'keepering can be on a do-it-yourself or amateur basis. Although gamekeeping at all levels is tiring and time-consuming, the pleasure derived from managing and improving a shoot often proves to be more satisfying and enjoyable than the actual shooting. Also the sport takes on a new all the year round dimension instead of the dozen or so days in a season that the average syndicate gun might expect.

There are many different types of game shoot and on low ground there is great variation, from the open partridge country to woodland areas where pheasants and woodcock may form the major part of the bag. Where water is available there may be scope for some inland wildfowling. The habitat and game-holding cover will dictate what sort of shoot can be developed, but variety in the species and countryside is a great asset to producing interesting days.

The objectives

For any new shoot starting from scratch the first step, whether a single individual or a group of people are involved, should be to identify and define the main objectives and to do so within the known limitations – be they moral, physical, or financial.

Is rough shooting, driven shooting, or a mixture of the two preferred?

Would the team want to lay on a day at weekly, fortnightly, or monthly intervals?

Is the primary purpose to provide sport for the members alone, or do the individuals wish to have the opportunity to invite guests?

Will such guests always be safe and responsible?

Do all the members of a syndicate wish to share in the work and essential duties of do-it-yourself ''keepering'?

Would it be more effective and more realistic to appoint two or three of the most enthusiastic as 'worker' members while the remaining 'drones' dig a little deeper into their pockets?

Are the guns so tied by business commitments that the employment of a professional gamekeeper is required?

What is the communal concept of a successful day and a suitable bag?

If a specific shoot is under consideration, all these questions and many others besides should be asked and satisfactorily answered before even embarking on a survey of the area, and before deciding on a management plan. It is sad how often ventures end in unhappiness because the original direction and objectives were never adequately clarified. This is especially liable to be the case where more than one person shares in the operation and costs of a shoot.

Undulating country gives greatest potential for testing shooting.

Considerations for choosing the ground

For those searching for a shoot or an area to develop into one, but with none of the team living on the ground under consideration, distance from the 'keepering force is one of the most important factors. Apart from the more obvious point that a shoot in the care of an absentee 'keeper is extremely susceptible to being poached, the cost of transport to and from the shoot can quickly accumulate to a massive figure. There is no doubt that to be most effective even the amateur should visit the ground every day, especially at the key times of year for predator control, releasing – if that is deemed necessary – feeding, and of course when poaching is likely. By law, most traps must be visited daily and birds in release pens must have frequent attention to be certain that all is well, while regular feeding always pays dividends.

The actual acreage of land available is not necessarily important. The suitable game-holding habitat is a far more critical factor. The famous Tower Hill shoot of Archie Coates of a mere ten acres which, with amateur 'keepering, produces two driven pheasant days (including spectacular lunches) is witness to this.

The sort of information that must be gathered in order to assess the potential can be obtained by observation on thorough walking of the ground, perhaps with

Belts, copses and spinneys are more valuable than large blocks of woodland.

Fig.1 A reasonable field size, interspersed with a hedgerow network, small warm manageable woods, and some water are among the habitat features which should make for a successful game shoot.

the help of a consultant, and enquiring of the owners, farmers, and locals. Is the land undulating? Are the woods warm and manageable? Does the farm have a southern aspect? Is the cover on the neighbouring shoots better? Is the farming system sympathetic to game and wildlife? Will it be possible to grow special cover crops? Would thinning of the tree canopy in some woods be allowed? Can the stock be fenced out of the coverts? The answer to these and related questions determine the value of the shooting rights.

Owning or renting and local co-operation

Anyone who owns an area of land suitable for development as a shoot has a number of advantages over those who have to rent their sporting rights. This is especially the case if they live on the shoot, for resident owners are able to keep an eye on events from home. This has far-reaching implications for most aspects of game management, but in particular, security.

The owner will normally be anxious to take measures to improve the game and wildlife habitat, and be more prepared to engage in long term conservation measures like planting trees and shrubs, thinning woods, even digging ponds – improvements that may take several years to produce results. Special game crop areas are frequently impossible to organise on an intensive farm where the shooting is rented, whereas the owner only has his conscience and possibly his farm manager to convince.

If the manager or foreman enjoys shooting it is a wise move to invite him to join the team, even if only for a day or as a walking gun. Big shoots on rented ground may arrange a special day for their tenant farmers, for without their co-operation running a shoot can be very difficult. Their help, together with that of the farm

4

staff, can revolutionise results. If the efforts to woo such 'locals' has succeeded it is surprising how soon the results show. Suddenly tail corn which has traditionally been burnt or tipped in a wood may be bagged up so that it can be of use for feeding; offers to check traps, join the beating line, look out for strange cars etc. come flooding in. These are the sort of signs that indicate one is on the road to success.

Renting or taking shooting rights

If a suitable area of land has been located and the owner is willing to let there are various ways in which the shooting rights can be made available. Payment itself can be in cash, kind, or indeed conditions. For example, certain quantities of dead game may have to be handed over or agricultural pests may require control as part of the rent.

It is most important to try to obtain an Agreement or Lease in writing because verbal arrangements are so often misinterpreted. It is valuable to have a formal document for either party to refer to if and when necessary, even if it has not been drawn up by a solicitor. It also may be useful to circulate a copy to all the members of a syndicate.

If the ground shows any potential for development as a shoot a long lease should be sought. The enthusiastic sportsman/conservationist is constantly investing considerable time and cash into improving the natural habitat for game. Often these efforts take time to show results and there is little future in this expenditure of labour and money or building up a stock of birds on a shoot that may pass into other hands the following season. Farmers themselves are the traditional custodians of the land and they or the landowner will often approve of the concept of judicious planting, coppicing or whatever such steps the shooting tenant is likely to want to put into effect for the future benefit of game and wildlife. Consequently they may be prepared to offer a reasonable length of lease.

Of course, personalities may clash and therefore a seven-year lease with a break clause at the end of the first is possibly the ideal situation for both sides to such an agreement. This should provide for a season during which the shooting tenant gets to know the ground and can explore and learn more about its real potential, while the owner has a chance to assess how responsible the new tenant is.

There are a number of points which should be included when actually drawing up the terms of any letting. The full names and addresses of the two parties concerned, the lessor and lessee, should be recorded, but it is usually simpler in the case of a syndicate merely to name the 'Captain'.

The exact area concerned should be described, including farmland, woodland, marsh and water, clearly stating any places that are out of bounds. It is extremely valuable to have a map of the area with the boundaries shown, together with the public roads, bridle paths and footpaths. In some cases farm buildings suitable for rearing may be included, while on bigger shoots a small acreage of grass may be required for rearing in the spring and summer months. If a professional 'keeper is to be employed a cottage may be included in the lease. In this case the party responsible for upkeep and repairs should be stated.

Leases commonly commence on the first day of the close season, February 2nd, and run for one or more years. Break clauses and the option to renew should be recorded, together with the length of notice required to terminate the lease by either party and possibly what conditions constitute reasonable grounds for premature termination.

The annual rent should be stated and intervals at which rent reviews are to be held. Rent can be index-linked and certainly this system avoids the ghastly shock of the massive rise that can result in triannual re-assessments, particularly in periods of high inflation. Linking to the responsible tenant concept already described, an increasing sliding scale of rent is sometimes agreed on the grounds that the shoot is gradually being improved by the mutual efforts of landlord and tenant. The actual cash is customarily due by February 2nd with a 10% deposit paid beforehand. Occasionally, half-payment in February with the remainder required on September 1st is allowed. The shooting tenant is normally responsible for paying shooting rates where they are applicable. (See 'Where will the money go?' on page 7).

Special conditions are sometimes imposed and these should also be recorded in writing. Access to and through the shoot and the coverts may be restricted, possibly only for selected times of the year. It may be that the shoot itself would wish to have certain restrictions imposed during key periods, for example during partridge releasing, when disturbance can be critical. It is certainly necessary to ascertain who else apart from the owner or farmer have access to the various areas concerned.

Responsibility for pest and predator control is normally a condition of a sporting lease, and if so the shoot may be liable for excessive crop damage by the creatures for which it has been given responsibility. The owner or farmer may also retain rights to control agricultural vermin, either by himself or for some of his staff.

Deer management and control may be included or excluded in a shooting lease and this should be clearly stated. Again this will normally include responsibility for any crop damage by deer.

In hunting areas the owner may wish to ensure access for the hounds, in which case this can be written into the agreement. The shoot tenants may suggest particular periods of the year when (or areas from which) the hunt may not be welcome. On the majority of large shoots and at most times of the year there is little harm the hunt should do to game as long as the pack and the field are under control, be they stag, fox, mink hounds, beagles or harriers. The main worries are likely to be on partridge ground in the autumn and especially on a very small shoot with limited cover.

Occasionally the owner may wish to retain one or more guns in the shoot or the right to carry a gun over the area or part of it when he wishes. This should result in a reduced rent, but such conditions should be stated clearly in the lease.

On a large shoot the employment of one or more 'keepers may be included as a condition and sometimes a minimum or maximum limit is placed on the number of birds that may be released. If this is so it must be recorded, including the species concerned. In practice it is often difficult for the lessor to check on such undertakings.

Again on the big shoot it may be advantageous to include conditions of notice on farm or estate management plans, particularly of actions in the woodlands. Felling, thinning, brashing, weeding, and planting plans may have enormous implications for the shoot, as will the timing of these operations. Similarly, advanced knowledge of agricultural cropping plans may be of great value, especially on a partridge shoot.

Certain areas of special game strips may be included in an agreement, in which case a maximum acreage might be agreed. If the cost of such crops is not included in the rent then the price that the shoot is expected to pay per acre should be stated.

The right to sub-let the shoot for a season or more and the option to sell individual days or even guns are, on occasions, not allowed. These are increasingly popular ways of recovering some of the shoot management costs and so it is vital to ascertain and record the position on these matters.

Most shoots insure themselves against accidents in the field with regard to gun safety, but in addition it may be a condition that insurance be taken out against damage to stock and crops. In practice this is a wise precaution anyway.

Finally it is customary for the tenant to have to keep accurate records of both pest and predator numbers taken, together with the game bags, all of which may have to be submitted to the owner annually or even more frequently.

Where will the money go?

Shooting, including game shooting, is no longer restricted to those with a deep pocket. It is true that a day at the driven grouse would devastate the average weekly wage packet but it should be possible for anyone to save up sufficient funds for an afternoon's walking up – for grouse the major expense could possibly be travelling to the moor. The chance to shoot at most gamebirds and wildfowl in Britain can be obtained at reasonable cost to the enthusiast.

However, when deciding how much of the shoot budget should be devoted to the various essential management items, the newcomer is often in the dark. The Game Conservancy have been conducting a survey of shoot accounts for over ten years. A mixture of full and part-time 'keepered shoots is included, so the findings may be of help to any novice shoot manager.

Some of the costs cannot be altered easily. For a rented shoot a figure will probably have been negotiated, possibly with a sliding scale for future years, to take account of inflation if a long lease is involved. In England and Wales, if the farmer and shooter are two different people, then sporting rates are levied. In Scotland they are levied regardless.

Table showing the Proportion of Gross Expenditure Used on Each Major Production Cost. (From the Game Conservancy *Game Shooting* Cost Analysis Figures)

	Expressed as a Percentage of Gross Costs.
Rent and Rates	8.3%
Keeping	34.0%
Equipment	2.9%
Restocking	24.0%
Winter Feed	18.9%
Game Crops	3.5%
Beaters	8.4%
	100.0%

These figures are a three year average from a sample of rented shoots.

'Keepering commonly comprises the largest single cost except where amateurs are giving their time. Even then if transport to, from, and around the shoot is taken into account, the real cost is often much higher than is realised. 'Time is money' and it is only by deriving pleasure from the actual gamekeeping that the part-timer can really justify the hours working on the shoot. The professional may require accomodation, transport and some of the standard perks such as free coal, electricity, telephone, dogfood and a certain amount of special clothing. Nevertheless, if the amateur alternatives do not live on or very near the area expenditure on the paid man may well be a sound investment.

The ideal situation is perhaps when a tractor driver, stockman, woodman or someone already working on the land has a few hours spare each day, at the critical times of year, which can be devoted to tending to the game enterprise. Living and working on the area is a most important advantage and such a person is normally well worth enrolling into the ''keepering force' either as an amateur or a professional.

Many shoots have an extraordinary aversion to buying sufficient good quality equipment for the various essential game management practices. Whether it be traps, rearing units, sections, release pens, chain saws or even a simple spade, if it is necessary or helps with an important job it is well worth purchasing. The cost of most capital items should be depreciated over a period of years and this soon makes it obvious that the investments have been worthwhile. In game management a poorly completed or part done job usually results in disaster, be it through increased predation, disease, or for any one of the multitude of other possible causes. Certainly savings on tools and equipment are generally false economies.

Rent, rates, 'keeping and equipment can all in a sense be included in the fixed costs of running a shoot. Once the level of operation has been decided they should vary relatively little. The remaining items can be regarded as the variable costs, where the scope for alteration even during a particular season can be considerable.

Where restocking with reared birds is practised a decision must be made about numbers of pheasants, partridges or duck that will be released. This is affected by the holding cover, the conditions on the ground and by the size of the shoot purse. The actual cost will also depend on the method of production, whether poults ready for release are purchased directly from a game farm, day-olds are bought in and reared on the shoot, or the whole process of egg production, incubation, and rearing is undertaken. As a further alternative it is often possible to pen laying stock and then exchange eggs for day-olds with another shoot or a game farm with spare incubation capacity. The common rate is for two eggs to be supplied for each day-old returned, with sometimes an additional cash payment for the job of hatching. Certainly for the small shoot it is often a mistake to become over-involved in the intricacies of reared bird production, especially if this is likely to result in less attention being paid to the more basic preparations of ensuring suitable habitat and controlling predators.

Fig.2 For a small or part-time keepered shoot it may pay to avoid mechanical incubation. Many different aged batches of birds are produced, not to mention the time involved in setting and hatching eggs.

(Left) The cost of special game crops may be justified by their ability to hold more game or show better birds.

(Right) It is the prime duty of all who shoot game to ensure that there are sufficient dogs and handlers to account for any wounded birds.

One of the most frequent errors encountered by Game Conservancy consultants when advising new shoots which are just starting is the initial decision to spend too high a proportion of the budget on birds for release. This invariably leaves inadequate funds remaining to provide the necessary conditions for these birds to acclimatise correctly to the wild.

The provision of sufficient winter feed to attract and hold game is important in this respect. As a rough guide pheasants may consume about 16 cwts of wheat per 100 birds during the entire length of the season if feeding starts about harvest time and continues into March the following year. With wheat costing £120 per ton it is important to avoid wastage and the use of straw on feed rides not only helps to draw pheasants but also reduces robbing by pigeons, rooks, and small birds. The cost of a few bales soon pays dividends in both respects. For ducks, poorer quality corn can be used, tail barley being one of their favourites. Fifty mallard can easily consume a bucketful in an evening. Partridges can be fed on cracked or second-quality wheat. Indeed some 'keepers prefer a few weed seeds in the sample. Partridges also eat significantly less than pheasants so in terms of winter feed they are definitely cheaper. However, where cereals are grown it should be ascertained whether the farmer objects to 'dirty' corn being put out, especially on field boundaries. Even in woods birds fed weed seeds may deposit them back on the land in their droppings.

The farmer will have been consulted as to whether any special crops can be grown for game. There may be an agreed acreage included in the rent or there might be areas difficult to cultivate profitably for the farm which can be planted for game. Otherwise a sum for loss of agricultural income must be allowed in addition to the cultivation, seed and fertilizer costs for any game crops. The actual figure will vary according to the quality of the land, and also to the awkwardness of the site. The smaller do-it-yourself shoots often feel that they cannot afford to pay the farmer for a special strip, but if it is likely to result in a significant increase in the bag or the quality of the presentation, it may be money well spent.

If driven shooting is included then cash may have to be reserved for the hiring of beaters. Particularly for partridge driving some experienced professionals are often valuable on the flank and in the line. There are a number of ways to save money when laying on a formal day which is primarily for pheasants or mixed quarry. Extra guns can be invited which will reduce the cost per head. The number of beaters may be reduced if half the guns take turns to walk in the beating line and then stand in the gunline. The beaters may be remunerated in kind, with a day's shooting at some stage during the season, with dead game, and with lunch. Lastly, willing wives, friends and children can be substituted for some of the professionals. This is sometimes a false economy unless sufficient of the team know the ground and exactly where they are trying to drive birds, and have the skills that the job requires. A misplaced stop, a beater that wanders out of line at an important moment, can so easily wreck a drive. Safety must also be remembered.

Transport for guns and helpers on shoot days may involve further cost unless it is possible to walk the entire area. Finally, pickers-up are of particular importance. It is the prime duty of anyone who enjoys shooting to ensure that there are sufficient dogs and handlers to account for any wounded birds as quickly as possible. In practice, professional pickers-up invariably pay for themselves in terms of extra birds in the bag.

Having added up these costs a total figure will be produced. For many shoots this may be the net cost which requires dividing amongst the parties concerned. With luck there may be some revenue from sale of surplus game, venison carcasses, pigeons, hares or rabbits. Possibly some income may be derived by producing extra chicks or poults to sell from the rearing operation. There may be some income from a let day. By subtracting such revenues from the total cost figure the net amount will be derived which, when divided among the number of participants, will reveal the actual cost per gun. This sum, the subscription, is normally payable to the shoot captain or treasurer by February 1st, or half on that day and the remainder on September or October 1st. The first instalment is obviously required not just as a deposit but because much of the expenditure in running a shoot is incurred long before the shooting season.

A useful system to raise extra capital on a shoot just starting, where initial expenditure is likely to be high, is to charge an entry fee in addition to the annual subscription. This fee can be used to purchase essential equipment which should last for a number of years. If any gun decides to drop out of the shoot at the end of a season he may be refunded all or part of the entry fee because his replacement will have to produce his or her joining sum.

The subscriptions of guns to a shoot may be liable to V.A.T. This should only be the case when the operation is run as a business. If it can be shown that a loss or at least no profit is made, but that the participants are contributing towards the running costs, all should be well on current evidence.

KIRKLEY HALL

Headings to help shoot budgeting

Costs per year

Rent Paid	Include V.A.T. and rent for any rearing fields or sheds.
Rates	Sporting rates if applicable.
Keepering	Wages including N.I. contributions and/or payments for additional part-time help.
	Housing – annual rent of property together with repairs and maintenance.
	Dogs – cost of dog food, vet, etc.
	Sundries – special clothing, cartridges for pest control, and other extras.
	Transport – depreciation of vehicle together with fuel, tax, insurance and repairs.
Equipment	Often more realistic for a new shoot to include all traps, incubators, rearing equipment, pens, feeders, hoppers, for five years and average out for each successive season.

These costs can to an extent be regarded as fixed once a certain level of operation has been decided. The remainder are very much more variable depending on the scale of the shoot and, in particular, restocking numbers.

Re-stocking	Egg production	– laying pen food
		– bought in eggs
	Chick production	– broody hens/food
		– incubator running costs
		– custom hatching
		– bought in chicks
	Poult production	– rearing food – crumbs
		pellets
		grain
		– heat for brooder – gas
		electricity
		paraffin
		– drugs and sundries
		– bought in poults
Winter Feed (post release period)	Pellets	
	Grain	
	Straw	
	Batteries for automatic feeders	

| Game Crops | Rent of ground or payment for loss of agricultural crops |
| | Seed, cultivation and fertilizer |

Beaters and	Payments to
Pickers Up	Beer and Lunches*
	Transport on shoot (tractor and trailer, etc.)

The addition of these items should produce a gross cost figure.

Possible income sources (not from subscriptions):

Sale of surplus eggs, chicks, poults.
Sale of rabbits, pigeons, etc.
Sale of dead game.

By subtracting this income a net cost of producing shooting should be produced, which may then be divided among the members in the case of a syndicate.

*Lunches and refreshments for beaters, pickers-up and helpers are often considered essential costs to laying on the shoot days.

Planning the programme

One of the most enjoyable parts of running a shoot is preparing a plan of operations for the year and then putting it into practice. It is particularly satisfying if one is in a do-it-yourself 'keepering situation and therefore able to see the fruits of one's own labours develop. When managing game and wildlife, as with gardening and farming, it is essential to work with the seasons and this can best be achieved by considering the resources available at the different times of year.

Cash, or lack of it, is often thought to be the limiting factor on many shoots but, having decided on the 'keepering system, labour is often more important. When planning and budgeting for the coming season in January or February, it is easy to think how simple and enjoyable it will be to feed the birds each day from July onwards. When the time comes, holidays, business commitments, and even illness, can radically alter the situation. It therefore pays in the first instance not to be over-ambitious on the expectation of a part-time labour force. It is possible, of course, if cash is not short, to buy extra labour at critical times, but gamebirds, like most stock, do not respond well to changes in the people tending to them.

Before considering cash or labour, the most decisive factor controlling how a shoot should operate will be the amount of suitable game habitat. For partridges, the agricultural system and cropping pattern and, in particular, the distribution of hedgerows and spring and autumn cover will influence the scope. For pheasants, the level of operation will be dictated more by the winter holding cover, warmth and shelter of the woodlands, and whether there are to be any suitable game crops on the ground. Of course, the latter can be specially established but normally the compensation required for the loss of the agricultural crop will make this an expensive option. In the long term, it is much more cost effective to work on the less profitable scrub and woodland areas to ensure that they have been developed to the best advantage for producing, holding and showing game.

Having established what resources – finance, labour and suitable cover – are likely to be available throughout the year the decision can be taken as to whether to concentrate on encouraging wild birds to prosper or whether restocking with reared birds will be necessary to ensure some sport. Should one develop the pheasant shooting first or aim to produce a mixed bag with partridges or even duck or waders as well? Certainly many smaller shoots would be well advised in the early years to concentrate their limited resources on developing the ground and ensuring that predators are adequately controlled throughout the spring and summer rather than becoming involved in the intricacies of egg production, incubation and rearing. If restocking is necessary there is much to be said for devoting the spring and summer to improving the habitat, protecting wild game from its natural enemies and buying in poults ready to release from a game farm. This system at least ensures that the ground should be suitably prepared for any birds that are to be released.

2 Taking Stock

Catching up pheasants

When starting or taking over a new shoot, even when there is plenty of stock, it is often wise not to catch up. Obviously hens in the laying pens cannot be hatching out wild broods, although if released early enough (by early June) they may lay a small clutch on the shoot and raise a few young. More significant is the time consumed catching birds, penning them for egg production, and in particular in egg collection, storage and possibly incubation. However, if laying pens or suitable equipment to construct them is available it may be worth catching up - especially in the wetter grass-growing areas where there is a big silage acreage - in order to produce eggs for incubation, sale, or swapping for day-olds or poults with another shoot or game farm.

All too often, catching up is left until shooting is over. Ideally, it should be completed as early as possible. It is quicker and easier to catch from a large population, and there will be less 'pricked' or injured birds which may produce infertile eggs. For this reason, some shoots and most game farms actually over-winter their laying stock in captivity.

It is advisable to put out and bait the catchers some time before they are to be set, using wheat or the grain to which the birds have been accustomed. According to the type of catcher, the number of hens available, and how many are required, the operation may take anything from a few days to several weeks. Much depends on the weather because in hard conditions birds will come to the feeds more readily.

There are two types of catcher - individual and multiple. The most common single catch trap is the 'basket' type, which is made from a few hazel rods. Alternatively an old broody coop can be used, or a shallow pit of 25 cm (10 in.) or so deep can be dug and a board employed. All these types are propped up on trip sticks, just high enough to allow a pheasant to walk underneath.

Single catcher tripping devices normally consist either of a springy wire or a bendy thin branch set so as to release the lid, coop or basket the moment the bird touches it. A strong wind can trip the mechanism if it is set too light.

Multiple catchers usually work on the lobster-pot principle, with ground-level funnels. Most will take half a dozen or more birds at a time. They can be made from a number of different materials but wire netting is liable to damage caught birds as they thrash about trying to escape. This can be minimised if catchers are not large (reducing the pheasant's ability for movement) and if they are visited

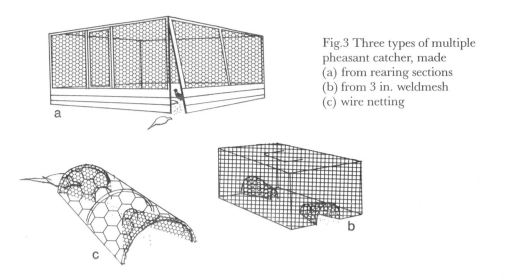

Fig.3 Three types of multiple
pheasant catcher, made
(a) from rearing sections
(b) from 3 in. weldmesh
(c) wire netting

a

c

b

frequently. If wire is to be used in the construction then 7·5 cm (3 in.) weldmesh
can be recommended because it makes a simple multiple catcher where the risk
of injury is considerably reduced.

Alternatively, a slatted timber type should be safe. The 'cage' can be about 1.2–2
m (4–6 ft) square so that it can be readily transported. The space between the slats
should allow the pheasant's head to pass through without damage. At each end
an opening about 0.5 m (1 ft) high should be left so that the pheasants can walk
in and out. After a suitable period of pre-baiting the wire netting funnels can be
slipped into the open ends. Such a catcher will hold half a dozen or more birds
with ease, and a sliding door will facilitate removal of those trapped.

If available, a rook cage trap with ground entrances can double as a pheasant
catcher. Also rearing sections are sometimes tied together to make a suitable
device.

It is most important that all birds are carefully examined for signs of injury or
disease. Only those in first-class condition should be retained for laying.

(Left) Setting a hazel basket catcher.

(Right) Weldmesh catcher. After a suitable period of pre-baiting, the wire netting
funnels can be inserted.

The chukar redleg, *Alectoris chukar*, has a black 'dog collar' and no speckling below on the chest.

Catching up partridges

Grey partridges, once they have experience of life in the wild, are difficult to keep calm in captivity. Furthermore, egg production is significantly poorer after their first laying season so it is important to know the ages of birds caught.

Redleg partridges by contrast often lay better in their second and succeeding seasons than in their first. In addition, if redlegs have been released on the shoot in recent years it is quite likely that they may be Chukar, *Alectoris chukar*, or Chukar crosses. Game Conservancy research over a number of years has shown that these birds, although they lay eggs and hatch chicks, rarely rear many young which survive to maturity in the wild. This is because the chicks have a very different diet to that of the 'pure' redleg, *Alectoris rufa*.

If the chances of wild production from birds left on the ground is slim then it is obviously sensible to catch them up and artificially incubate the eggs and rear the young to an age when they can be released with a reasonable chance of acclimatising to the wild.

Another factor is that the territory size of redleg pairs is generally much greater than that of the native greys. It can be in the region of 25 ha. (60 acres) on a modern British farm. Often after shooting there are still a great many more birds on the ground than there are suitable territories. This is frequently the case where redlegs are released and so it may pay to catch up a proportion of them for egg production purposes.

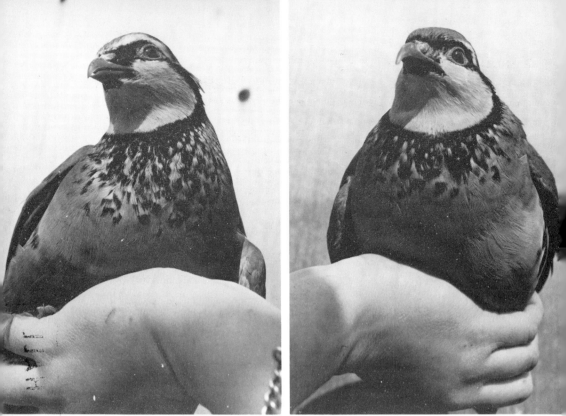

(Left) Pure redlegs, *Alectoris rufa,* have a black speckling which extends well down the chest.

(Right) *Rufa-chukar,* the cross bred, exhibits some of both characteristics.

Ideally this should be done long before February, although on a well-stocked pheasant shoot it may be difficult to keep pheasants out of the catchers in December and January when their numbers on the ground are still high. A pheasant catcher can be successfully used to catch redlegs, but if the birds have been fed on hoppers it may pay to use a multiple catcher deliberately designed to be set in conjunction with them. Alternatively, a catcher made from sections can be very effective where birds have been released earlier in the season from pens made out of them.

Partridge catchers should be visited especially frequently for two reasons. The birds are wilder and more prone to panic than pheasants and also, if they do become startled in the catcher, their amazing ability to spring in the air and accelerate over short distances can lead to the captives injuring themselves in a short space of time.

Being a covey bird it is often possible to catch large numbers very quickly. Once one bird goes into the trap its fellow covey-mates will frequently all follow. For this reason single bird catchers are not to be recommended.

Penning partridges for egg production

Penning partridges for egg production may seem an ambitious step, particularly for the normal farm shoot, but it can prove a lucrative exercise. The price of both redleg and grey partridge eggs, chicks and poults is much higher than that of pheasants. The food consumption is generally less and the egg numbers normally produced by the 'pure' redlegs at 30 per pair and by greys at 35–40 is broadly comparable with that of the pheasant. Chukar and Chukar cross can lay significantly more eggs, up to 100 per pair, so the profit margins can be very high. Producing partridge eggs on the shoot or even in the back garden can therefore yield useful cash. If releasing partridges, a big saving can be made on restocking costs.

It is unlikely that the do-it-yourself 'keepered shoot would wish to become involved in the capital outlay and labour requirement to produce partridge eggs from paired systems. For grey partridges, pairing (or possibly using trios) is essential for egg production. With redlegs, paired birds produce the most eggs, but for the average shoot, flock mating is a much simpler, cheaper and a less time-consuming operation.

The paired pens used by the 'serious' partridge egg producers are normally made with wire floors which have the great advantage in reducing the risk of disease. However, if suitable fresh grass ground is likely to be available each spring, pairing on grass can also be successful. The pens are commonly made in batteries and should be at least ½ m by 1½ m (18 in. by 5ft) for each redleg pair but, in the Game Conservancy trials unit, it has been found that greys lay better in a pen of at least twice that width. Each unit should contain a feeding and watering area, a soft roof-netted open area and a laying box, normally filled with sand.

If just a few eggs are required, perhaps to set under broody bantams, then the traditional 3 m by 2 m (10 ft by 6 ft) movable pen or something similar made from sections will be adequate for pairs of redlegs or greys. A simple way of making a pair pen is to nail a length of corrugated iron to each side of a broody coop. An end piece and some soft netting on the roof makes a very cheap and simple movable pen of ½ m (18 in.) in width. The length is dictated by the size of the iron sheet.

The most common situation is where it is intended to produce redleg eggs from overwintered or caught up birds. Luckily this is possible by flock penning the birds. Trials at Fordingbridge have shown that one cock to three hens is an adequate ratio to ensure good fertility. Space is also an important consideration and a pen of 10 m (30 ft) square is the minimum size for 25–30 birds. Some cover in the form of fir branches will be appreciated but it is also wise to make some baffles of hessian, or to place bales or hurdles across the pen. These enable the cocks to keep out of sight of another aggressive male and also prevent birds flying at speed and then crashing into the side wire. The provision of some shelters with sand or dry earth underneath will be popular as a dusting area. They can also help to keep eggs

(Left) Partridge pair pens are usually built in batteries on a wire floor to reduce disease risk. N.B. Greys need more space than redlegs.

(Right) Sexing redlegs by weighing birds in a bag with spring balance gives reasonable accuracy. N.B. The plastic bag is used only for the photo: hessian is recommended.

clean if they are used as laying places.

In addition to the saving in terms of capital outlay and servicing, the communal type of pen avoids the necessity of being absolutely certain of the sex of birds when pairing. The cock redleg normally has a false spur or nobble on the back of the leg while the hen does not. For pure redlegs, *A. rufa*, the cocks generally exceed 525 grammes (18½ oz.) while the hens seldom attain such weight. A suitable sized loose woven hessian bag with a draw string and a spring balance are all that is required. These methods should be adequate to ensure reasonable accuracy for someone with experience, but the novice is bound to make the occasional error. In pair pens, two cocks penned (if they do not fight to the death) lay no eggs, while two hens may lay an impressive number but, of course, fertility would be disastrous!

Redlegs should be penned for laying by the middle of February. Greys should be paired up and penned earlier during a cold spell in January, and certainly by February 1st.

Sexing grey partridges is considerably simpler than redlegs, the shoulder feathers of the cock bird not having the characteristic creamy white cross bars of the hen.

Penning a pheasant laying stock

Where pheasants have been held over-winter or caught up early – before the end of shooting – they will probably have been kept in special aviaries. By the end of

February they should be transferred to the laying quarters so that they have a full month to settle before their first eggs appear. If hens have been caught after shooting it may be possible to move them directly to the laying pens, but where a fixed unit is used it is important that they do not foul the ground and destroy the grass in the cold, wet winter weather.

There are three basic systems of penning pheasants for egg production. The simplest is to place six to nine hens and one cock in a standard, covered movable pen. This is a little smaller than the ideal for the number of birds and a pen made up from rearing sections to 3 m (10 ft) square is still light enough for one person to shift but will enclose nearly double the area. The main advantage of a movable pen system is that fresh ground can regularly be made available. Pens should be set out with enough space between them to allow for the necessary moves. Obviously such units take a little more time to service than fewer, larger pens.

At the other end of the scale, open-topped communal pens should use less man hours per day to manage – providing the eggs can be found without difficulty. Such pens are also cheaper to build in terms of cost per bird accommodated. However, to limit the danger of the ground vegetation being exhausted during laying, an area of about 65 m (70 yds) square is required to pen one hundred hens and the accompanying ten or so cocks. Ideally, light land, a southern aspect, good shelter, and a tough grass sward are required. Adequate shelters and cover should be included. This can easily be provided in the form of fir boughs, branches, corrugated iron arcs, and feed staddles.

The birds must be prevented from flying. If they are going to be liberated before July, it is important not to wing-clip them. Instead they can be brailed – which involves binding the innermost and outermost joints of one wing with tape or special leather brails. One problem that can arise and become serious in an open-topped pen is egg eating. With many pheasants in the pen it is not easy to isolate the culprits. Furthermore, if there are any crows, magpies, rooks, or jackdaws in the area they may soon be robbing the pen of both eggs and food. Small birds such

(Left) A 3 m (10 ft) square movable pen is suitable for a cock and a harem of six to nine hens.

(Right) A tough grass sward, free draining land, and plenty of shelter are required for a communal pheasant laying pen.

as sparrows and starlings may also quickly learn to plunder the breeders' pellets.

Consequently some shoots use an 'in between' system, making pens of at least 10 m (30 ft) square to take twenty hens and three cocks. A net can be placed over such a fixed run. If egg eating breaks out among the pheasants it should at least be easy to identify the offenders. If there are sufficient sections to place individual cocks with a harem of the customary seven or so hens in a fixed unit this will probably produce more eggs per hen, but a minimum area of 12 m by 3 m (40 ft by 10 ft) for each group is required. The extra equipment and labour involved in penning 'family' groups may be justified by the significantly greater egg production over the season. From mid-April to late May, when a communal pen might produce 20 to 25 settable eggs per hen, the one cock and harem pen, whether fixed or movable, may yield 35 to 40 eggs per hen.

In an attempt to reduce the likelihood of egg eating breaking out some 'keepers find it useful to place a few hard stone dummy eggs in the pen a week or so before laying is due to commence. It often seems to be curiosity that starts the vice, but once initiated it can spread rapidly, therefore prevention is infinitely preferable to cure. The idea is that any potential culprits will be put off by their attempts on the dummies. If a bout of egg eating does break out the old-fashioned preventive of putting mustard or diesel in a pecked egg may have an effect, but it is probably better to watch the pen carefully and remove any offenders immediately they are spotted. If time does not allow watching, a dye can be placed in an egg so that it leaves a tell-tale mark on the culprit. Unfortunately, many birds will peck at an opened egg but it is the initial breaker that it is so important to isolate.

All cock pheasants should have their spurs removed at penning so that they do not inflict any damage to their hens while treading. The ideal tool for this is an electric debeaker which singes and cauterizes as it cuts. If birds show any signs of feather picking a light debeaking or application of size C (large) bits should be made immediately. Some people take one of these measures as a matter of course. The fitting of 'specs' is practised by some 'keepers in an attempt to prevent or stop egg eating and/or feather picking. There is no doubt that these can sorely stress birds, especially if they are fitted to caught up stock. The inability to see ahead of them is such a handicap when first fitted that many professional game farmers consider these devices should be avoided. Good stockmanship and careful management of the breeding stock should make them unnecessary.

It must be remembered that egg laying requires considerable energy expenditure on the part of the hens. To ensure the best possible chance of good production of fertile eggs with good hatchability a correct balanced diet must be fed. At the very latest, birds should be in their laying quarters by March 1st in the south. Also by this time they should have been gradually changed from their maintenance ration onto breeders' pellets only. There should be little harm in throwing greenstuffs such as kale or bolted cabbages into the pen, but special additives such as oyster shell grit or extra vitamins should not be provided. They may serve to disrupt the manufacturer's very carefully planned balanced diet.

One month before egg laying is the ideal time to worm the laying stock. Provided this is done well in advance of the first egg then most of the available compounds with the exception of 'Gapex' can be used. If a problem occurs during laying then 'Mebenvet' or 'Wormex' are two formulations available that have been tested and found not to depress egg production in themselves.

Eggs – collection, cleaning and storage

On a recently started, small, or part-time 'keepered shoot, there is a strong case to avoid becoming involved in the intricacies of incubation. There are all sorts of snags, ranging from the variable results often produced by small machines to the headache of rearing and releasing a multitude of different aged birds.

If a game farmer or nearby shoot can be persuaded to accept eggs throughout the laying season and in return supply day-olds or poults in suitable sized batches for restocking, then the arguments in favour of egg production are quite different. Also if a stock of sitting type bantams or hens are available, a few eggs may be produced from penned stock to supply clutches for broody incubation and rearing. This is particularly suitable for producing a few 'coveys' of grey partridges.

In the south of England the first pheasant eggs should appear in early April while the first grey and redleg partridge eggs are not often laid until the end of the month. Chukar and Chukar crosses can begin as early as February. Eggs from pens on the ground should be collected at least once a day. Pheasants tend to lay in the afternoon and so an evening pick up is the most important. Ideally they should be collected more often; at 10.00 am, mid-afternoon and early evening. The shell of an egg left on the ground can be penetrated by bacteria in as little as three hours. If the egg is warmed by the hot sun, the embryo may begin to develop, upsetting subsequent growth. Early in the season eggs left out overnight may be chilled and frosted. Frequent collections during the day will also reduce losses from egg eating, and as mentioned, in an unroofed pen predation by corvids can be catastrophic.

For collecting from movable pens, a bamboo cane with a small egg net made from a wire loop and nylon stocking end is handy for extracting eggs without disturbing the birds. A soft plastic bucket makes a good container for carrying eggs, and it is important to ensure that no hairline cracks are caused.

Because of the speed at which eggs may become contaminated, cleaning should be carried out immediately after collection. Clean and dirty eggs should be separated and the worst given a preliminary scrub with wire wool or clean plain paper. All eggs may then be immersed and washed in an egg sanitisor, such as Nusan II. Three minutes at a temperature of 43°C (110°F) is sufficient to sterilise the surface without bacteria or chemicals being absorbed through the shell. Thermostatically controlled washers are very efficient for those handling large

23

numbers. Plastic coated wire buckets allow the rapid draining and drying that is desirable.

Eggs of unusual size, shape, shell thickness, colour, or with rough surfaces or cracks should be discarded. Normally this may be 10% of the total. Storage is important. A dark cool room with a steady temperature and a little ventilation and dampness is required; 13-15°C (55-60°F) is about right. The eggs should be placed in trays, small end down. If they are to be kept more than a few days these would be tilted by placing a block of wood at one edge, and alternating edges each day.

Pheasant and grey partridge eggs should not be stored for more than a week, especially if they are going to be machine incubated, because hatchability is likely to suffer, even when care has been taken over the conditions. Redleg eggs, by contrast, seem to suffer much less and will hatch well after a fortnight's saving, although this is not to be recommended. It is important to keep duck eggs in a separate place from those of gamebirds because they often carry disease which may be passed on.

For a hatchery there are disease risks in accepting eggs from outside sources either for swapping into day-olds or poults or for custom hatching. Correct collection, cleaning and storage should at least minimise these risks.

Mallard – catching up and laying pens

Mallard are generally caught up with little difficulty on or near a water area where they have been regularly fed. However, Game Conservancy trials have shown that 'truly wild' birds will often produce infertile eggs. This resulted even when 'wild' drakes were paired with a managed strain of ducks.

Most of the multiple catchers which work, on the walk-in funnel principle described for pheasants, will be successful for mallard. Once again pre-baiting is the key to success. For ducks that are a little nervous it is sometimes more effective to use a floating catcher rather than try to induce the birds to feed on land. A

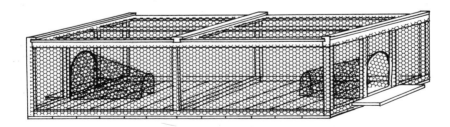

Fig.4 A multiple duck catcher which can be floated or set at the water's edge.

simple frame made up from planking or even an old door will suffice as the basic raft. A compound at least 45 cm (1½ ft) tall and covering most of the base should be made from wire netting or weld mesh. At least part of this should be 5 cm (2 in.) mesh so that small birds are not trapped. At one or both ends a removable funnel tapering from 33 cm (1 ft) down to 12 cm (5 in.) should be made. It is useful to provide a lid in the top for easy removal of the captives. Expanded polystyrene wired underneath makes good buoyancy material.

The catcher should be baited and floated near the normal feeding area with no funnels for a period until the ducks are thoroughly familiar with it. The food supply elsewhere is stopped so that the birds are encouraged to eat the catcher bait. If there are plenty of mallard available from which to catch it may be a matter of minutes before the duck enter the catcher and so the operation can be very quick, with a minimum of stress to the birds themselves. Catching up duck for egg production may offer a convenient opportunity to cull surplus drakes on a farm pond where too many randy males can be a nuisance by chasing and chivvying the nesting females during incubation and when they have broods.

Mallard can be successfully penned for laying in a number of ways. Sex ratios, in a large pen, of as few as one drake to ten ducks have given satisfactory fertility, but a drake to three or four ducks is more usual in small pens of twenty or so birds. Pens can be open-topped if the birds are prevented from flying, but again there may be a danger of egg predation from corvids. Happily, the mallard themselves don't eat their eggs. In a topped pen an area 10 m (30 ft) square is large enough for about twenty birds, and water should be provided. Mallard prefer to perform the mating act, treading, on water. Baking trays, or sinks let into the ground will suffice. However, when ducks and water are involved in a pen, the result is normally the rapid production of a messy, muddy patch. If there is a pond nearby, part of the bank and a small section of the water area could be penned.

Laying mallard may be fed on grain initially but breeder's pellets should be gradually introduced to the diet until no corn is fed by the beginning of March, about a month before the first eggs are likely to appear.

Eggs invariably become dirty in the muddy conditions, but as most laying is before 9.00 a.m. picking up an hour or so after this will be ideal. It is well worth providing some artificial laying sites and a number of 25 litre (5 gallon) drums with one end cut open and one third buried in the ground will prove popular. Very muddy eggs may need to be dry-cleaned with wire wool before washing, and storage is similar to that of pheasants. Sometimes people fumigate duck eggs because they can carry bacteria which may develop into a problem during incubation.

Fertility is usually high (90%) in mallard eggs produced from managed stock in laying pens. Over the months of April and May, the peak production period, between 40 and 50 eggs can be expected from each duck.

Inland wildfowl – encouraging nesting success in the wild

Any shoot with a water area may have the potential to produce duck. Regular feeding may draw in a flight from the local population, supplemented by some winter migrants. Dusk flighting can provide some of the most exciting sport but often releasing any number of mallard onto such a river, pond, or lake can wreck the system. The reared birds will often bully their wild cousins and chase them away or merely eat all the food before the wild duck arrive each evening. The result is that evening flighting is often all 'take' and no 'put back' – a situation which most game conservationists and shooting people are not happy to entertain.

The mallard is basically a ground nester although hay stacks, and the boles, branch junctions, and holes in trees are frequently tenanted. Predation is therefore an important factor in nesting success and over the long potential laying period, which can extend from January to July or even later, eggs and incubating females are at high risk to winged and ground vermin. However, duck will readily nest over water and this habit can be used to provide virtually ground-predator-proof artificial nesting quarters.

The Dutch have for centuries been weaving special nesting baskets from reed. These are mounted on stakes driven into the bed of the water area and lined with

Mallard often need encouraging to use nesting baskets. Placing them on the ground initially can do the trick.

Once duck are familiar with nesting in baskets these may be set up on sticks over the water. A little hay can encourage duck.

a little dry grass. However, in Britain it appears that mallard require education before they can be persuaded to use the baskets. One system is to rear a few ducks with baskets in close proximity so that they become used to them. The other method is to lay a few baskets on the ground, leaving the nest eggs and incubating duck at risk – again until the female mallard finds and becomes familiar with them. Once trained, the future generations gradually appear to get the message, and thereafter it should be possible to place the baskets on stakes over the water with reasonable prospects that they will attract the right tenants. However, it should be remembered that Holland is a country with carefully controlled water levels which suits the use of fixed stakes. The big rise in levels that is common in some parts of Great Britain may flood the basket and the eggs of its occupant.

Consequently, for areas with fluctuating depths it pays to construct rafts. For larger water areas these should be substantial. The original Game Conservancy design used two 5 m (15 ft) lengths of telegraph pole held 1.5 m (5 ft) apart by angle-iron struts and a board bottom. After discovering that 200 litre (40 gallon) drums perish after a few years, sacks of expanded polystyrene protected from duck damage by wire netting were employed for flotation. The trough of the raft is filled with straw which makes a suitable medium in which to plant rushes as natural camouflage. Finally the outfit is launched and towed to its moorings on the water and a suitable nesting box is fitted to each corner.

A very cheap artificial nesting place can be made from a 25 litre (5 gallon) drum by cutting a hole in one end and laying it on its side about one-third full of earth. However, even when painted this can look rather shoddy and will do little to grace an attractive pond. A simple and reasonably priced alternative is to make a 30 cm (1 ft) square box out of slab wood (off-cuts) which can be obtained from any sawmill. The rough bark edges give a natural look. An important addition is a small porch about 15 cm (6 in.) square to hide the nest, eggs, or incubating duck from passing eyes. These boxes and the raft will float up and down with the water level and in a short time take on the appearance of a natural island. Mallard seem to be rather more prepared to take up a nesting tenancy in the boxes than to occupy baskets, while occasionally a tufted duck will lay in the rushes between the boxes. Coots and moorhens are also inclined to take up residence.

However, regular inspection of the artificial nest sites is required not only to dissuade unwanted squatters but also to remove early mallard eggs. The system induces particularly early laying but even in the south a mallard duckling has little chance of survival if it hatches before mid-April and usually it will be May before there is sufficient suitable insect life. The system of picking up the early eggs for

Rafts can be made into natural looking islands for nesting boxes where water levels fluctuate. Duck tend to lay earlier in artificial nest sites. Eggs may be collected until the end of March if the offspring are to be released.

artificial incubation was technically illegal under the new Wildlife and Countryside Act, but the Department of the Environment has since issued a general licence. This permits the owner or occupier or a person appointed by him to pick up mallard eggs until the end of March in England and Wales and up to the 10th April in Scotland provided that they are hatched, reared, and released back into the wild.

Although there can be difficulties in persuading mallard to use such nesting places when provided, the results if these problems have been overcome can be dramatic. The population on one gravel pit near Fordingbridge was transformed from two breeding pairs to thirty-five in just one season! The eggs in such artificial nest sites are difficult, if not impossible, for winged predators to see for the ten-day to two-week laying period, and when the duck comes off to feed during the 28 days of incubation. The clutch is also safe from most ground vermin with the notable exception of mink and the most hardy fox or rat. The attentions of over-randy drakes, which quite often disrupt incubating ducks, can also be reduced if not totally avoided because the girls are virtually invisible in either box or basket.

The result of such conditions should be a much greater than normal nesting success with large numbers of ducklings produced at a time when 'fertile' waters should have an adequate supply of suitable insect food. However, where recently made wetlands or acid waters prevail this essential duckling nutrition may not be available in sufficient quantities to give a good chance of survival. If this is so it may not be wise to provide the nesting facilities and attract breeding mallard to such an unsuitable place. Alternatively, it is possible to provide the required nutrients artificially through custom milled poultry or game chick foods.

The main danger when trying to feed mallard ducklings is that the greedy parents will eat all the crumb food provided. This can be overcome by providing a creep feed system. All that is required is some 7.5 cm (3 in.) weldmesh and an old door. By making a cage framework of the former over a section of the latter a floating feeder is produced. This should be placed either on the banks or launched onto the water area with some food nearby to attract the broods. The main area where the high protein mash or crumb is placed inside the weldmesh should only be accessible to the young ducklings. Once they are too fat to squeeze through the mesh they should be past their most vulnerable stage and hopefully will then learn to find natural foods for themselves.

3 Predator Control (I)

Why, when and what?

All British gamebirds are ground nesters. Anyone taking on responsibility for a shoot should be aware that a systematic and determined campaign to reduce predators just before the breeding season can be crucial to successful wild game production. Later in the year continued control in and around any releasing areas is essential to protect birds during the acclimatisation period.

The operations are basically seasonal. Hours devoted to trapping vermin in the autumn are often wasted. Most of the enemies of game are territorial and therefore if controlled in the autumn may be replaced before the following spring.

Predator control is an emotive subject, and there are extremists on both sides of the fence. The majority of modern gamekeepers are extremely good field naturalists and are not out to kill the last of any species, as some of their predecessors may have been. Tolerance and a live-and-let-live attitude is increasingly common, but there are, unfortunately, a few rotten apples in every barrel. Many townsfolk seem to be completely unaware of the benefits that conserving game has for a multitude of non-quarry wildlife species.

Gamekeepers and shoot managers are normally convinced by their own experience of the effect that predator control has on the production of their quarry species, but there are few scientific studies that prove the point. Consequently, the Game Conservancy has recently embarked on a research project to assess the results of the current legal techniques performed correctly on game and wildlife populations. Every gardener and farmer knows only too well that to grow a good crop the 'weeds' must be kept under control. The intention should be to tip 'the balance of nature' in favour of the crop at the crucial periods. This should be the precise intention of good game management.

The gun, the trap, the snare, gasses and even poisons are among the armoury that may be used for certain specified pest species. Basically all birds are protected except game-birds and some ducks and waders (which have certain close seasons), some pest species such as the pigeon, starling and sparrow and the corvids (apart from the raven and chough) together with some gulls, moorhens and coots. All birds of prey are protected. Of the predatory mammals most can be legally controlled unless specifically protected like the badger, otter, pine marten and polecat. This means that the fox, feral cat, mink, feral ferret, stoat, weasel, grey squirrel and rat – the main mammalian threats to game – are lawful targets.

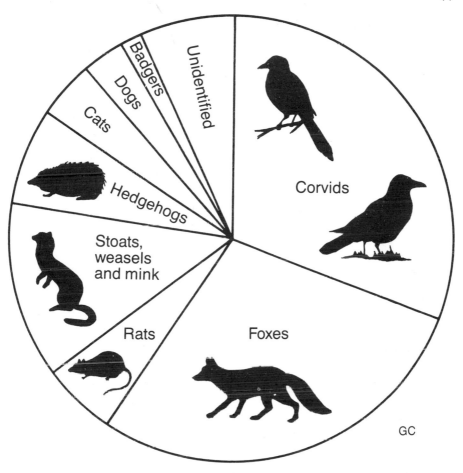

Fig.5 The Game Conservancy's pheasant nest recording scheme, 1977-79: proportions of pheasants' nests lost to various predators.

The gun and driving

The gun can prove an important part of pest and predator control on the shoot. In particular, the part-timer may find difficulty in making the necessary daily inspection of a trapline, and therefore be forced to rely more on firepower.

In late winter and early spring cover is at its lowest after frost, wind, and snow have flattened annual vegetation. This is the ideal time to conduct any organised vermin shoots. After the shooting season there should be little disturbance to game, and with a matter of just a few weeks to go before the first gamebird eggs appear, this is the optimum period for predator control to be effective. It may also be a useful opportunity to give beaters and helpers a chance to have a shoot.

Dog

Fox

Stoat

Badger (protected)
(front)

Mink

Rat

Cat

Grey squirrel

Fig.6 Easily recognisable footprints of some mammalian game predators. As drawn, they are approximately two-thirds in size.

Safety is a subject which should be stressed, particularly where people who don't shoot regularly are involved. What may or may not be shot must be made abundantly clear. If any dogs are included in the line it may be necessary to restrict the shooting of ground game and predators or insist that dogs are put on leads at certain stages.

Standing guns are normally positioned down wind of the walking line and in places such as rides, where clear shots are presented and where predators are known to customarily make their escape from the coverts.

Unless a specified predator is known to be in an area vermin drives are often partially for sport. Although a good number of pests and enemies of game may be accounted for, this cannot be regarded as effective control.

Grey squirrel – drey poking

One pest which is particularly suitable for a special shoot is the grey squirrel. Not only are they egg eaters and robbers of the feed ride, but these relative newcomers to Great Britain can devastate young trees, especially sycamore and beech. They breed in February and again in April. Therefore, poking out the dreys at this time of year can be an effective way of destroying squirrels, in addition to providing a sporting day out.

A cold, wet and windy day should confine most squirrels to their quarters and give the best results. A useful squirrel hunting team requires three or more people – one or two with the drey poking poles, and two or more with guns to shoot the evicted squirrels. In suitable woodland bags of seventy or more in a day are not unusual.

The poles are sectional rods, made of a light aluminium alloy, and a standard set gives a maximum extension of about 20 m (60 ft). Further poles can be added but controlling greater length can prove a problem for the inexperienced. In some areas it is possible to borrow a set of poles from the M.A.F.F. Wildlife and Storage Biology Department.

New dreys can be recognised by the state of the leaf which the twigs bear, but old dreys with withered leaves may hold a large number of occupants, particularly in winter. It is essential to poke the dreys out thoroughly so that any young will fall to the ground. If the dreys are completely destroyed rather than just damaged, only new dreys will be in evidence the following season, and the operation will be much quicker. One or two likely lower dreys can be left as 'testers' and may yield many squirrels throughout the year. A few light prods with a long stick left permanently by the tree will flush the tenants. During the main drey poking operation all old magpie, crow, and other unwanted corvid nests should be destroyed.

Three simple points should always be remembered. Be careful with metal poles near high tension cables. Never shoot at a squirrel running down a tree. In such

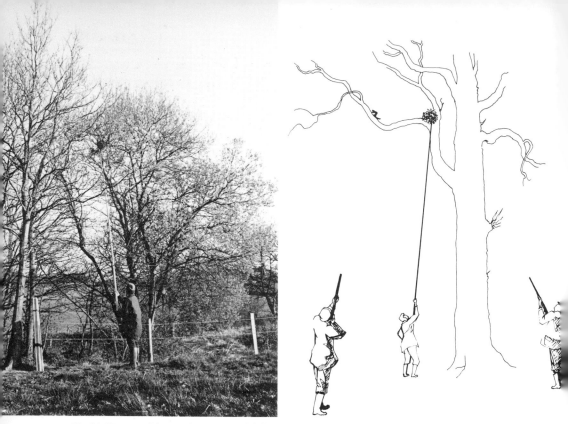

(Left) Drey poking poles are useful for pushing out corvid nests before the leaf is on the tree.

(Right) Fig.7 At least three people are required for grey squirrel drey poking; one operates the poles, the others position themselves on either side of the tree.

a situation the animal should be allowed to run outside the 'gun circle' before a shot is fired. Also always remember to count the number of poles when moving from one drey in search of the next. A single lost pole can take hours to find in a large wood.

Drey poking can account for a good number of squirrels and provide exciting sport for the team. It can also prove an excellent way of teaching young shots safety and an opportunity to test their markmanship. However, as a comprehensive method of pest control, it is not total and it should therefore be used in conjunction with other methods, namely, the trap and baiting with the warfarin type anti-coagulant poisons.

Corvid control

As soon as the first game-bird eggs appear each spring, crows, magpies, rooks, jackdaws, and even the occasional jay, begin the search for these nutritious meals.

The control of corvids is therefore important prior to the nesting season. The only legal methods are shooting and cage trapping. Crows and magpies are the worst offenders at damaging breeding birds because they do not just take eggs but also nestlings. Both have been observed killing chicks, and on occasions not requiring or bothering to carry away the corpses. The important point is that although the egg stealing of rooks can be very serious at least the parent gamebirds may have the opportunity to lay another clutch if the first attempt is predated. It may be that this delay results in the chicks hatching later in the year when the weather may be warmer and the necessary insects for chick food more abundant. When gamebirds lose chicks to predation the situation is far more serious because it is rare for them to nest again that season. Even when they do the delay is frequently so great that the young do not survive well.

Neither the magpie nor the crow are communal nesters and their breeding period may be spread over several weeks, therefore control with the gun requires care and attention.

Decoying, calling and nest stalking

All the corvid species can be lured within range of the gun by decoying or calling. In particular their habit of mobbing raptors can be used to advantage. A stuffed owl placed in a prominent position in a woodland ride can attract a crowd of screeching jays in a very short time. It may pay to leave the jays, which inflict significantly less damage to nesting game, and wait for the more menacing magpie or crow to join in the jostling. Plastic owls can be purchased at most gunshops and even in huge unrealistic sizes can be successful. Stuffed or imitation ferrets, cats and foxes can all be similarly effective. It is, of course, illegal to use a tethered live decoy.

Another way to attract corvids is by calling. There are a number of different predator calls and the crow call which when blown makes the characteristic 'caw' has been successfully tested by the Game Conservancy advisory staff. It is most effective in the spring when the crows' territorial instincts are at their peak. The 'rabbit squeal' calls designed to attract stoats and foxes can also draw magpies and crows. One of the simplest methods of luring a nearby magpie is to shake a part-full box of matches. Often, this simulated chattering noise is enough to entice any magpie within hearing to investigate.

Any new corvid nests seen appearing in hedgerows, copses or woods, should have their position noted because once the tree leaf is fully out they will be more difficult to discover. If any magpie or crow proceeds to the incubation stage, then there should be opportunities to stalk the sitting birds. Two people make the operation easier in that both sides of the nest tree can be covered to prevent escape. Alternatively, an ambush may be set, but again more than one person is required. Crows can see incredibly well, but fortunately their mathematics is limited. They

(Left) Stuffed or plastic decoys of crows or owls can be used to lure corvids within range of the gun.

(Right) Rooks can be inveterate egg thieves.

cannot count. Therefore, if two people walk up to a nest and the impatient parent crows see one walk away, it should not be long before they return to 'face the music'. In some areas 'keepers consider three people are needed with two departing ostentatiously to leave the nest apparently safe. Perhaps crows are becoming even brighter!

The rookery

Rooks not only damage wild game production on shoots by thieving eggs, but they can also inflict serious damage to game food strips and sometimes even farm crops. Maize is very prone to being attacked both in the spring at the drilling and seedling stages, and in the autumn when the crops ripen.

Rooks are communal nesters, traditionally preferring elms. It was at one time thought that the heavy losses of these copse and hedgerow trees in the last fifteen years due to Dutch Elm Disease might seriously reduce rook numbers. It appears that they are adaptable birds because they have learnt to set up breeding colonies in ash, beech, oak, and even pine trees. They are among the first birds to build in the spring and in most parts will have laid and be sitting by early April. From this situation a method of control is possible.

The object is to continually disturb the rooks on a cold frosty night after incubation has started and when the embryo in the egg has begun development.

A string of agricultural bangers is tied inside a large metal drum which has had one end removed. Locals living near the site of the rookery should be informed out of courtesy that there will be some bangs during the night and it may be advisable to inform the local police. A rope should be slung up into the branches of the rookery so that the drum with the lit fuse can be pulled up among the nests just as dusk is falling. Every twenty minutes or so a banger should explode and the noise amplified by the drum, resonates around the rookery causing sitting birds to lift off their nests. If the correct night has been chosen the eggs will be chilled. After an extended incubation period the parents finally seem to become disenchanted with the lack of hatching success.

With no young to feed the parents should not have to hunt so hard for eggs and other food, which should restrict potential damage to nesting game. Perhaps more significantly, when this system was under trial by the Game Conservancy on local Hampshire and Wiltshire shoots it was found that after two years, and sometimes after only one, the rooks gave up the particular site and colonised another patch of trees for nesting.

Some people are unaware of the damage rooks can do, and certainly on occasions they can be beneficial to agriculture, particularly when feeding on one of their favourite delicacies, the leather jacket. On one shoot where the Euston system was practised and wooden dummy eggs were placed by the gamekeepers in gamebird nests while the real things were artificially incubated the evidence was all too obvious. When the 'keepers went to thin the young rooks out in early May, there at the base of the trees the ground was found to be littered with the dummies. The adult rooks had robbed both partridge and pheasant nests to feed their nestlings, but had finally dropped the wooden replicas when they could not crack through their shells!

Branchers

The second week in May is recognised as the peak period in the south of Britain for shooting young rooks. On a fine, sunny evening, the fledglings move out of the nest to the surrounding branches before making their first attempts at flying.

Normally a good number of 'branchers', as they are called, can be accounted for with the gun. This can hardly be called a testing sport, but certainly it can help to curtail rapid expansion of numbers in the rookery. With a breeze, shooting with a .22 rifle can be interesting and, if a few young rooks have fledged, they can provide an ideal situation to instruct the novice shooter in safety as well as shotgun marksmanship. It might be added that there are some who find the young rook, cooked together with gammon or steak, a treat for the palate.

On a fine evening in early May, rook fledglings can be controlled when they move out from the nest onto the surrounding branches.

Cage trapping corvids

The other legal method of taking members of the crow family is by cage trapping. This can work at any time of the year, but is most effective when the targets are either hungry or have families to feed. Baits will vary according to local conditions and the season.

The most common cage trap is the funnel type, which can be of almost any size and works on the lobster pot principle. In Game Conservancy trials, the ground entrances proved the most popular way in, but if grain baits are used, gamebirds may be caught. A door of about 0.6 m (2 ft) width will give access to the trapper and a perch is required across the roof funnel, which should be at least 0.5 m (18 in.) in diameter at the top tapering down to about 20 cm. (8 in.) at the bottom. The wire mesh should be 40 mm (1½ in.) to avoid catching small birds although rooks and crows will be contained in 50 mm (2 in.) netting, but magpies and jackdaws will not.

Because corvids rapidly realise the effects of cage traps, they need to be moved fairly frequently. They should therefore be constructed in sections which may be quickly dismantled. There are two variations on the funnel type. The 'rook pen' has a roof made from 100 mm (4 in.) sheep netting. Rooks drop down into the cage through the large mesh, but are unable to fly out. Jackdaws and magpies can

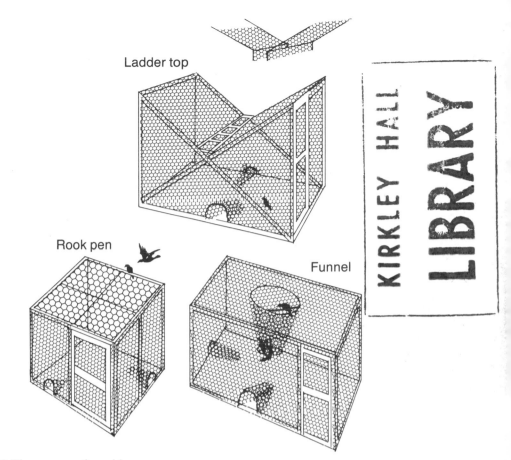

Ladder top

Rook pen

Funnel

Fig.8 Three types of corvid cage trap.

escape. The ladder-top cage has proved very successful. A V-shaped roof slopes down to a ladder of 15 cm (6 in.) width which runs the length of the cage. These rungs of the ladder are about 22 cm (9 in.) apart and hanging wire netting curtains together with blocked off end rungs prevent birds escaping by climbing out.

Pre-baiting is the key to success. Bait should be scattered all around the cage and ideally the roof should be left off and the door open with some food inside for this period. White bread, eggs, slit-open rabbits, dead sheep, and corn, have all proved successful. In hard weather, corvids often congregate around stock-feeding areas. This situation can be capitalised on by introducing a trap and using the same stock feed as bait after the sheep and cattle have been moved. A decoy in the cage can be helpful but it must be remembered that food, water, and some shelter must be provided by law. The trap must be visited daily and care should be taken to dispatch victims humanely and if possible unobtrusively so that other unconvinced birds are not warned away.

Cage trapping is unlikely in itself to give adequate control of avian egg

On sheep ground a carcass can prove an effective bait for cage trapping crows.

predators. However, the advisory staff of the Game Conservacy have instructed many clients on how to start a successful campaign. The most impressive authentic report back was where two cages in two months accounted for over 900 jackdaws, rooks, crows and magpies, and some other pests including a few grey squirrels.

4 Predator Control (II)

Small ground predators and spring traps

Throughout the British Isles there are a number of small ground predators which can take eggs, chicks, and sometimes even adult game. Again, the main period when damage is likely to be significant is during the spring when game is breeding and when the predators themselves have families of young to feed. A few species are considered sufficiently rare to warrant protection, such as the otter, polecat and pine marten. Although common in many counties the badger is also protected. However, other mustelids – the stoat, the weasel and the mink, all most efficient hunter/killers, may be controlled. Also the occasional escaped ferret can wreak havoc particularly to captive game or poultry. The rat and the grey squirrel are omniverous and can inflict considerable agricultural and forestry damage respectively but both are also partial to eggs and nestlings. The hedgehog, an egg predator, may no longer be taken by trapping.

When the harsh, cold conditions of winter begin to lift and the weather warms, activity increases in these creatures. They begin to move around more frequently, hunting out the likely areas for a kill and feed. Some are territorial and therefore have their beat to patrol against aggressors. Consequently, March is the month when control measures should be increased and, in particular, when the tunnel trapping campaign should be intensified.

In Great Britain, there are seven humane spring traps which have been officially approved for use against small ground vermin. All must be set under cover like their now illegal forbear, the gin trap. It was a tooth-jawed trap designed to hold rather than kill instantly, which is primarily why it was outlawed. However, in the days when it was used in large numbers by rabbit trappers, a heavy toll of ground predators was also taken, which was a great help to the game conserver.

A number of its replacements are no longer in production but, if available, they may still be used. The Lloyd trap looks similar to the gin but its jaws envelop its catch across the body, killing quickly by snapping the spine. The Sawyer, invented by the famous river-keeper, was a simple and deadly little trap for rats, stoats, and weasels, but it never became popular. The Imbra is primarily a rabbit trap but it will take small ground vermin. The other rabbit traps will all perform the dual function, but the Fenn rabbit trap never received M.A.F.F. approval for use except on rabbits.

Those currently manufactured are dominated by the Fenn range. The Mk IV rat trap is the main weapon with which most tunnels are armed, although its

41

Current approved humane spring traps are all designed to kill instantly.

predecessors in the series were equally effective. More recently the Mk VI was launched with the specific additional purpose of taking mink and also adult rabbits. In Game Conservancy field tests in 1982 it proved efficient in both respects, but its wider and more powerful jaws require a larger tunnel or hole than the Mk IV.

The last in the list is the Juby trap, which is a strong and large machine designed primarily for the rabbit. Many experienced operators consider it rather large and cumbersome, but if a big enough site can be found or made to accommodate its fearsome jaws, it should prove instantly deadly to even the most thick-set mink. Because of its particularly powerful spring there is a foot lever to assist in opening the trap.

The tunnels

The number of tunnels that will be in operation on the shoot during the important spring period will depend on the available cash to purchase traps and the area to be trapped. Probably, the most important limiting factor will be the time required to inspect and service the trap-round every single day, which is not only essential on humane grounds, but also a legal requirement.

As a guideline, a full-time 'keeper on 500–1000 hectares (1250–2500 acres) should be able to run between 70 and 100 tunnels. On a wild bird shoot, more

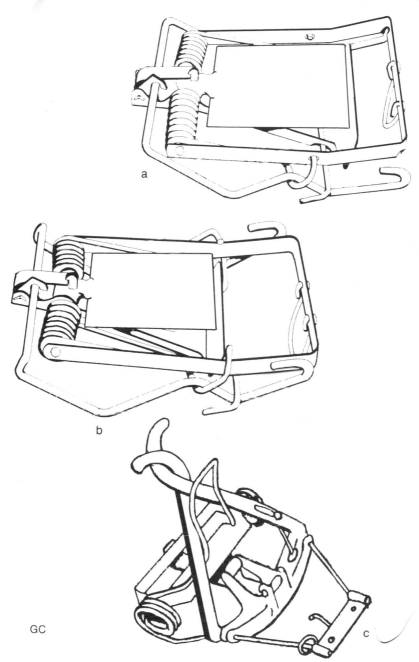

GC

Fig.9 The approved humane spring traps currently in production.
(a) Fenn Mark IV Rat Trap (shown open) for small ground vermin;
(b) Fenn Mark VI General Purpose Trap (shown open) for small ground vermin,
rabbits and mink;
(c) Juby Trap (shown closed) for small ground vermin, rabbits and mink.

43

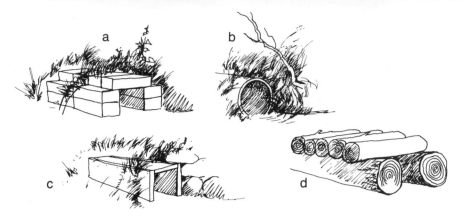

Fig.10 Materials successfully used to make tunnels.
(a) Bricks, or bricks and slate;
(b) 6 in. pipe (pitch-fibre ideal);
(c) 6 in. boards nailed together;
(d) cordwood or logs.

may be required to give adequate protection to nesting birds and, later in the year, their broods. The part-timer may be limited to a few dozen and even they may require a rota for inspection when 'communal 'keepering' is practised.

Obviously in this situation, the siting of tunnels is particularly important. Traps along farm-tracks, in gateways, over streams, might be on routes already travelled every day by farm staff, who would be prepared to check them. Accessibility is an all-important factor. However, it is equally vital to avoid sites close to public rights of way. Even among country dwellers, there are many who do not understand the need for pest and predator control. There are others who appear to enjoy deliberately sabotaging the work of those who are trying to manage game and wildlife. Trap stealing and vandalism becomes more common each year.

In order to find the best sites for catching there is no substitute for experience. Trial and error are the best instruction. It may pay therefore to make more tunnels than one has traps and to ring the changes. Often a site that catches well one year will not prove so successful in the following year. In choosing sites, one should try to think like a stoat or a rat and to imagine the sort of places that will attract the attentions of the curious, inquisitive predator.

Hedgerows, fencelines, ditches, banks, streamsides, planks over water-ways, are all classic places. This is hardly surprising, for these are the routes which connect the larger dwelling places of copse, crop, and covert for travelling vermin. Tunnels should take their toll if installed to lure the passer-by running these predator paths.

Materials for making the tunnels are legion. Most common is probably three 0.5 m (18 in.) to 0.7 m (2 ft) lengths of 15 cm (6 in.) board nailed together with a spacer to hold the sides apart at the correct distance. Where an old building has collapsed, an excellent tunnel can be made from a few bricks, possibly roofed with a piece of slate. 15 cm (6 in.) pipes, if sunk about one third into the ground, are ideal for the smaller Mark III Fenn but need modification to take the current Mark IV. A hole about the size of a 10p piece drilled in the side of a 15 cm (6 in.) pipe will accommodate the lump housing the safety and trigger catches of the larger Mark IV, allowing it to fit without rocking and to spring freely. The pitch-fibre pipe is particularly useful as it is very robust (nearly unbreakable!). It is very dark, which seems to be an inviting feature to many predators, and it is light and easy to carry in suitable lengths.

Of course, natural materials such as logs, stones or boulders can readily be converted into a suitable site, and have the advantage that they should blend in with the surroundings. Whatever is chosen for the construction, it is increasingly important to camouflage the tunnel with turves, sticks, leaves, rocks, or whatever will look right in the particular situation. This is not only to deceive the intended target of the trap but also to reduce the chance of the passer-by recognising the device.

It will pay to cut tracks leading to each entrance of the tunnel. This will help to funnel passing predators to the site, especially where there is a furrow alongside the trap route. If this can be blocked to make a deflection, then vermin running the furrow should be certain to pass through the intended place regardless of their natural curiosity.

It is this curiosity on which the tunnel trap plays. Few small ground predators can resist the temptation of a dark entrance with fresh earth and a natural looking 'track in'. In addition, it will often pay to set the occasional 'baited trap'. For this a blind-ending hole of suitable size to take the trap, such as in a bank, an old log pile or the base of a tree is ideal. Fresh rabbit liver, or something similarly appetising, makes an attractive draw particularly to a hard-hunting bitch stoat or weasel struggling to feed a young family. Alternatively, a normal tunnel can be baited, but this will require the setting of a trap at each end. Perhaps surprisingly, this baiting rarely makes a great difference to the catching success of a well-sited tunnel except possibly in a drainpipe under a bridge where rats are frequently encountered.

(Left) A couple of bales laid together can make a successful tunnel or baited trap site, especially in woodland or close to a feed ride.

(Right) It will pay to cut tracks from field boundaries into the tunnel entrances.

Setting and checking tunnel traps

Whichever of the legal humane traps is used, catches are more likely if they have been weathered. New, shiny, glinting metal and the smell of factory and grease may make many victims wary as they approach a tunnel. Therefore, when new traps are purchased, it pays to leave them outside and exposed to the elements for a few weeks before setting. Some 'keepers actually bury them in the hope that this will accelerate the tarnishing process. Dipping in a weak solution of vinegar can certainly be helpful in this respect.

Once suitably soiled, the trap can be set. The tunnel should have been installed for a little time and therefore have 'grown' into its surroundings.

Firstly, a little loose earth should be removed from the base of the tunnel so that the set trap sits flush with the level of the ground. The ring at the end of the chain should be secured by pegging into the surrounding mud or by stapling it to the tunnel. Larger predators, feral cats, foxes, badgers, and even dogs, can soon learn about free feeds from tunnels and it is costly if they remove the trap as well!

It must be remembered that the weasel in particular is a lightweight animal and therefore the trap should be set accordingly. A slight pressure on the plate should be sufficient to spring the device and when the occasional field mouse is caught, the trapper will know that he is setting fine enough. Once the trap has been slid carefully into the hollow scraped out of the base of the tunnel, the loose earth

A pair of stout sticks at both ends of the tunnel should reduce the chance of catching non-target animals, in particular dusting gamebirds.

should be pushed back to cover it. In some exhaustive Game Conservancy trials, traps that were lightly covered for camouflage did not catch any more than those left visible, but the risk of theft and vandalism is undoubtedly greater if the jaws and plate are conspicuous. When satisfied that the trap is suitably hidden, the safety catch must be taken off. Although painfully obvious, even the most experienced 'keeper will, at some time, have overlooked this elementary essential.

Because the trap site is surrounded by loose earth it may attract birds looking for a suitable dustbath. A pair of stout sticks at both ends of the tunnel should ensure that these do not become unintended victims, and, at the same time, may help direct the predator traffic over the plate of the waiting trap. For the big Mk VI, a larger tunnel is required although a restricted entrance may be used as well as, or instead of, sticking the ends. Since, as already stated, it is no longer legal to take hedgehogs by trapping, this precaution may also help to reduce the risk of their capture. The larger Imbra and Juby traps need a special tunnel split into two so that the jaws can open and close without fouling on the tunnel sides.

There are many tricks to the trapping trade. When a bitch weasel in season is taken, a little urine squeezed onto the plate of the traps may lure prospective mates to the site. Stoats are known to be funeral attenders and therefore a dead stoat left on a tunnel may attract another to its end. The hanging up of the victims of the trap as a gibbet nearby is sheer folly, however proud one is of the results of the control campaign, for it serves only to enrage those passers by who do not comprehend the countryside and the importance of pest and predator control.

If the traps are sufficient in number, well-sited and set and inspected regularly throughout the spring breeding period then the results will be evident during the following shooting season. More wildlife on the ground and more gamebirds in the coverts is a much more effective display of the results of predator control than a line of decaying corpses hanging from barbed wire or a tree branch.

The fox

The largest and possibly the most serious game predator in many areas of Britain is the fox. However, where both hunting and shooting are important country amenities, it is vital that there should be co-operation between the followers of each sport. As the acreage of huntable country shrinks, it is even more important that landowners allow the hunt access to their ground. Even on easily disturbed small acreage shoots it is often possible to offer opportunities for the hounds at cubbing and after the main shooting days. Equally, shooting folk and 'keepers must be allowed to control this most important of game predators, especially during the crucial spring and summer breeding season.

Foxes are, however, increasing in number in many places, from suburbia to Highland glens, and in some of these, hunting is impossible. Some traditionally fox-free areas in the Fens and Eastern Scotland famous for decades for their wild

47

Bushing up and gradually restricting rides can be effective at creating a suitable snare site for foxes.

game have now been colonised. If the numbers of corvids and foxes are not contained during the breeding season there is little hope of nesting success for wild birds nor is there much point in tunnel trapping for small ground predators.

There are three basic methods of fox control: shooting, gassing and snaring. Big cage traps may take the occasional urban fox which is accustomed to hunting around rubbish dumps, but in general it cannot be regarded as an effective method.

Shooting

Fox driving in late winter and early spring when the cover is down, if conducted carefully, can account for a few outlyers. Also, if a fox is known to be lying up in a certain cover, a drive contrived to quietly move the animal to strategically placed standing guns who are silent and downwind will often work. Considerable emphasis should be placed on safety. Heavy shot sizes from Nos. 3 to B.B.'s should be used, and only close shots for a certain kill should be taken.

It is also possible to draw foxes within range of a shotgun or rifle by 'calling'. Various devices are available to imitate the sound of a squealing rabbit or hare. Dawn and dusk are good times and after dark, foxes may come readily up a torch beam to the call. It is especially effective after 11.00 p.m., possibly because by then any hunting fox that has not made a kill is beginning to become hungry and the noise of a rabbit in distress may sound very appetising. An alternative attraction in late winter and early spring is a tape recording of fox mating calls.

It is most important to know the ground well when shooting at night, and to be aware of which fields contain farm stock. The normal procedure is to work upwind, calling a few times and then casting a high-powered torch beam around the area. If a fox is located the eyes should be illuminated and the light should be kept off the animal's foreground. A red filter appears to make the beam more acceptable to foxes which, with further calling, can at times be summoned up the beam to within a matter of yards. Provided that suitable weapons are used to ensure instant dispatch this is probably the most humane method available of killing foxes. Using a rabbit squeal-call, stoats, weasels, feral cats and even mink can be summoned by this system, which is best learnt by going out with someone already experienced.

48

Gassing

Cyanide gassing powders, such as Cymag, are effective for killing foxes in earths. However, on very light sandy ground problems may arise with the gas escaping through the pores of the soil. The powder should be carefully placed well down each entrance with a spoon mounted on a long stick. The holes should quickly be sealed with a plastic fertilizer bag followed by plenty of firmed down earth and turves. For safety, two people are necessary for this operation and care should be taken to work upwind of the gas. Where rabbits and rats are frequently controlled by gassing a farm may possess a hand or machine pump. These are more efficient, but a bigger team of operators may be required to ensure that all the entrances are sealed as soon as the powder is seen escaping from them.

Amyl nitrite is the antidote to cyanide poisoning and the special capsules of it should always be carried when gassing. A relatively new alternative to Cymag has been introduced called 'Phostoxin'. This would appear simpler and safer to use as it comes in tubes in pellet form so that one pellet can be placed down each hole and sealed in. Once a tube is opened all the pellets must be used.

From March to June vixens will move cubs about, and so known favourite earths must be regularly checked. This should be done with the necessary gassing equipment because the slightest hint of disturbance can cause the family to shift to new quarters.

As with shooting, anyone likely to be involved in gassing should first become thoroughly familiar with the techniques and safety precautions with the help of an experienced operator.

Snaring

Snaring is probably the most successful way of catching foxes and without it protection of livestock, particularly sheep at lambing, and game, would not be effective in many areas. However, snaring is not the most humane method of control. Skill, experience and fieldcraft are all required to become proficient. The object should be to catch foxes only, and to minimise suffering.

The wire is set in a pear-shape about 21 cm (8 in.) across and 15 cm (6 in.) deep. Only a free-running eye is legal. The bottom of the wire is normally set about 15 cm (6 in.) from the ground, the height of five fingers and an outstretched thumb, although this varies according to the situation of the run. A tealer or pricker, a blackthorn or hazel stick of 1.5 cm (¾ in.) thickness, split at one end, holds the snare in position over the run. Occasionally a second tealer may be used on the opposite side in a windy site. A stop, a few turns of plain wire, should be firmly squeezed onto the snare 20 cm (8 in.) from the eye so that it will not close any tighter. This ensures that no animals are accidentally caught by the foot or other parts of the anatomy.

Where deer are present a jump bar or leap consisting of a leafy branch supported by two forked sticks a few centimetres above the snare can persuade

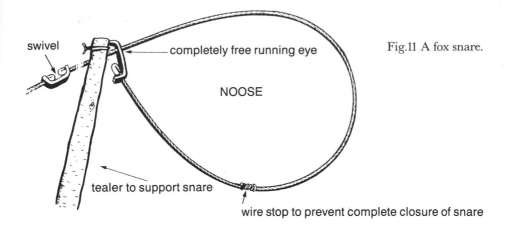

swivel

completely free running eye

Fig.11 A fox snare.

NOOSE

tealer to support snare

wire stop to prevent complete closure of snare

them to hop over it. Where the little Muntjac are present, leaps may not be effective. The wire should be secured via a swivel to a fixed point such as a stake at least 0.5 m (18 in.) long driven firmly into the ground or tied to a solid object. This can result in a good catching run being disturbed when a fox is caught so some 'keepers prefer to use a drag attachment. Something strong and at least the size of a fencing stake is required. The captive will usually make straight for the nearest cover where such a stake should be trapped. Snares should not be set under fencelines even when they reveal tell-tale signs of fox fur. Instead, they should be placed in the run leading to it where there is no opportunity for the victim to jump the fence when caught.

Anyone setting snares must follow certain procedures to minimise accidents: all snares must be inspected at least once a day (by law) and preferably at dawn; the correct strength wire with a swivel and adequate securing system must be used; snares should never be set close to public rights of way or where there is any risk of catching domestic animals, stock, or deer; they should always be lifted when hounds are meeting in the area.

It is easy to understand how opinions on predator control and, in particular, the fox, brings out emotional feeling, especially with wildlife photos of fluffy cubs being so appealing to the general public. Those who have had to control predators but have also seen nineteen partridge nests close to hatching taken in one night or a lamb part-eaten by a fox but left alive with a fretting ewe will understand both sides of the problem.

Feral cats

The cat that has learnt to hunt 'wild' in the countryside can do every bit as much damage to nesting game and chicks as the fox. It is sad that so often this situation is created by the thoughtless dumping of unwanted pets. The feral cat is a menace to wildlife, but fortunately having domestic origins it is relatively easy to take in a cage trap.

50

A simple design can be made up at home from wood, wire netting and some slates. It is important to make the trap plenty big enough because a cat that is only part in when the door drops and can escape is unlikely to make the same mistake again!

Suitable baits include fresh fish, rabbit liver or, if a particular cat is known to have been killing gamebirds, a dead one may do the trick. However, even for very wild 'moggies' tinned catfoods are normally the most successful. The advantage of a live catch trap is that should a particular pet be caught then there is the option to return it to its owner.

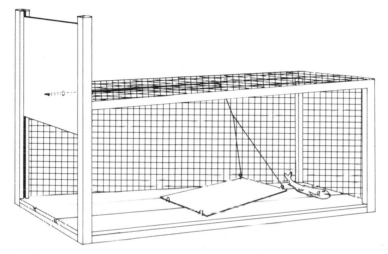

Fig.12 The Martin trap is simple to make and is an effective live catcher for feral cats. It should be at least 0.6 m (2 ft) long.

Cage trapping mink

Most of Great Britain is now colonised with feral mink. Some have escaped from fur farms, while others have been deliberately released by vandals allegedly in the cause of 'animal rights'. The fact remains that few areas are free from the potential dangers posed to game and wildlife from a very determined and efficient mustelid, which although particularly acclimatised to wetlands can prosper several miles from river, stream, lake or pond.

Mink are not often seen in the wild but fortunately their presence is relatively easy to detect. They leave a very characteristic footprint showing all five toes splayed out in astral form, much bigger than would be expected from an animal of such weight and size. Other classic signs of the presence of mink is a sudden reduction in the moorhen or watervole population. These are two top prey items.

Because they have come from ancestors that have been kept by humans in cages, mink are very bold, and cases are recorded of them attacking domestic stock and even people. Luckily this boldness and familiarity with cages makes them relatively easy to trap. Of course, mink may be taken in tunnel traps but the Ministry of Agriculture Wildlife Department have designed a cage trap that has proved even more effective. It is made of 14-gauge weldmesh: lighter mesh or bits of wood as part of the construction are simply not adequate to contain a strong male mink. The traps can be purchased complete or the materials for assembly can be bought much more cheaply.

Siting the cages is largely a matter of common sense and experience. Holes in riverbanks, hollow trees, paths across streams are the sort of spots likely to prove successful. Bait is not always necessary but fresh fish or rabbit liver are among the favourites. Whole families can be caught in the summer by setting several traps alongside one another. (After the loss of some pintail during breeding experiments at the Game Conservancy headquarters, seven mink were taken in one night in nine traps set alongside the duck pens). It is important to camouflage the cage, both to reduce human interference and to increase catching success. The trap should be secured to something solid and preferably with wire. Captured mink can make a considerable commotion and therefore on banks they may move the traps some distance, even toppling them into a river or pond.

Of course, cage traps catch predators live, and it is as well to remember that irate mink can inflict excruciating pain to any part of the anatomy that they are offered! The trap is therefore fitted with a handle. Do not immerse the trap and captive in the local pond, for mink are well adapted to water and take several minutes to drown. An air gun barrel poked into the cage will often be seized by the mouth of the mink and if care is taken to direct the shot through the brain then a swift humane end is ensured. A small-gauge shotgun may also be used, but great care is needed not to damage the trap.

Mink breed during the spring and early summer and can rear large families. Anyone wondering about the merits of leaving their mink until the autumn and winter when the pelts are in better condition in the hope of a fur coat for wife, girlfriend or mistress will be triply disappointed. Firstly, there is a multitude of

Sites along waterways are likely to prove successful for cage trapping mink.

different colours of mink; secondly, pelts from 'wild' specimens tend to be scratched and marked; and thirdly, by this time of year the mink will have wreaked their normal carnage on game and wildlife populations.

Rat control and poisoning

Most predators and pests do some good in one way or another, but it is difficult on a shoot to give any credit to the rat except perhaps to its amazing adaptability. Food crops, eggs, chicks, poults, even adult birds can be at risk.

Rats will be taken in tunnel traps, but often additional methods of control are required. Gassing as described for foxes can be a useful way to limit numbers where the holes of a bury are accessible, but this can be dangerous if practised near buildings.

Rats, mice and grey squirrels (in certain counties) are the only animals that it is legal to poison without special licence. A number of anti-coagulant compounds are available through retail outlets. They work on a cumulative basis, the victims continuing to feed until they die from a lethal dose, so it is important that sufficient bait is available for them to take the required quantities over a number of days.

The poisons can be purchased ready mixed or as a concentrate for adding to a cereal type pre-bait. Selection of pre-bait can be important because many animal foods contain vitamin K in sufficient levels to be a partial antidote to the anti-coagulants poisons.

Placing the bait in a situation so that it is not available to other animals, in particular pigs and dogs, is important. Also it should be under cover and off damp ground. Corrugated iron, tiles, sheets of board and pipes are all suitable. The poisons begin to have an effect after three to four days, when consumption should begin to decrease, but bait should be replenished until it ceases to be taken. A few days later a check should be made for signs of survivors of the blitz.

To deal with any new invasions of rats on farmland and to nip a possible build-up in the bud, permanent baiting points around the shoot area are to be

Sachets of rat poison in plastic bags should be placed under cover so that they are not accessible to other animals.

recommended. Special weatherproof containers can be purchased, so that they only require checking at monthly intervals. A 1 m (3 ft.) length of pitch-fibre pipe with a hole cut in the middle for a filling point can be made. It is important that a sound seal and lid be fitted to prevent rain seeping into the bait.

Another simple system is to make up sachets of poison in little self-seal plastic bags. These can be carried around the ground and distributed in dry places such as underneath corrugated iron sheet or in log piles where they are not accessible to other animals. The bag should keep the bait in good condition until it is gnawed open by a rat or mouse, both of which love chewing plastic.

Grey squirrel control with poison

The use of warfarin for grey squirrel control in England and Wales is defined in the Grey Squirrels (Warfarin) Order 1973 made under the Agriculture (Miscellaneous Provisions) Act 1972. This specifies the bait, poison concentration, method of presentation and counties in which warfarin may be used. Warfarin may not be used for squirrels in Scotland and there are limitations in a number of counties in England and Wales. These are designed to reduce any risks to other animals, in particular the red squirrel.

When setting out the hoppers the object should be to persuade as many squirrels as possible to start taking the bait quickly. An average density of a hopper to 4 hectares (10 acres) of woodland is normal. When first put out some unpoisoned pre-bait should be scattered around each site. Whole maize is good for this because it seems very attractive to squirrels and later it will be obvious if the poisoned wheat is spilt by accident. Hoppers must be firmly secured by pegging or weighing down under stones. Some camouflage is valuable to reduce the risk of interference, and it is important to ensure that the tunnel does not tilt down so that the bait can run to the entrance. In areas where the public have access it is advisable to have the word 'poison' clearly marked on each hopper.

The sites should be visited at least weekly to check the bait levels, at the same time ensuring that it is still able to flow freely from the container to the tunnel. A stick waggled about will usually clear any blockage, but care should be taken not to pull poisoned grain too far forward. Any spillage around the hopper should be removed. If large animals like badgers are pushing hoppers over then they should be set up on level tree branches or platforms may need to be made.

Evidence of success is when the poison is no longer being taken. A few days later the hoppers should be emptied or removed. Residual bait may be stored in a dry place in a labelled plastic bag.

The use of warfarin poisons to control both squirrels and rats can be thoroughly effective, and can prove a great saving in terms of time over other methods. However, as with all pest and predator control techniques, maximum efforts should always be made to ensure that the job is performed as carefully and as unobtrusively as possible. Being ostentatious will risk attracting the attentions of vandals and troublemakers, and, even worse, being careless will lead to non-pest species being put at risk.

Provisions of the 1973 order

Poison
: Warfarin:3-(α-acetonylbenzyl)-4-hydroxycoumarin or its soluble salts.

Concentration
: Not exceeding 0.02% weight warfarin/weight of bait.

Bait
: Whole grains of wheat over which the warfarin is evenly distributed.

Method of
Presentation:
: In a hopper made up of two components:

outside
buildings
: i. a tunnel not less than 230 mm long and not more than 100 mm internal diameter or internal square dimensions,
: ii. a container of any size or shape to hold the poisoned bait.

The container must be firmly attached to one end of the tunnel and securely closed when holding poisoned bait so that the bait is accessible only to animals which have entered and passed along the length of the tunnel. Access by an animal to the poisoned bait at the junction of tunnel and container must be at a gap not more than 20 mm high and no wider than the tunnel.

inside
buildings
: As for rat control.

Excluded
Counties
(except inside
buildings)
: Northumberland, Cumberland, Westmorland, Durham, Lancashire, Norfolk, East Suffolk, Isle of Wight, Anglesey, Caernarvon, Denbigh, Flint, Merioneth, Cardigan, Montgomery, Carmarthen. (Areas are those defined before the 1974 reorganisation).

Warfarin baiting hoppers for squirrels can be set up on planks or level tree branches in areas where there is a risk of animals like badgers pushing them over.

5 Crops for Game

The value of special crops for the shoot

Suitable game habitat is the primary requirement for a successful shoot. With agricultural systems continually intensifying it can be increasingly difficult to hold game on the modern farm. One of the biggest changes has been the shift towards more winter corn which has made autumn stubbles, a traditional favourite for holding game, something of a rarity. If land can be spared there are a number of special crops which can help to redress the balance.

The three prime purposes for which game crops are established are to help hold more birds on the shoot, to draw birds to an area where they can be presented in a particularly sporting manner, or to produce supplementary feeding for game. Cover is normally the most important factor and many crops do not provide any significant food. Kale, canary grass, artichokes, mustard, and fodder radish are all cover crops. Maize, buckwheat, sunflower, tic beans, millet, and wheat or barley are the crops commonly used to provide the food. Maize, sunflower, and millet have a limited range in Britain because of the warmth required for ripening. Also, after a period of hard weather, the cover these food crops afford game can be drastically reduced.

The Game Conservancy developed a number of different cocktails in the 1950s and '60s designed to produce food and cover, and many seed merchants now offer similar mixtures. However, they are often difficult to establish in that there is a host of different seed varieties and sizes. This makes drilling, as opposed to broadcasting, difficult and chemical weed control virtually impossible. For many crops, drilling is necessary to produce sufficient open ground between the plant rows for birds to move about freely. Dense, wet stands of crop are not normally favoured by game.

The size and shape of an area of crop are often critical to success. For shooting purposes, a strip is more satisfactory than a square or block because fewer beaters will be required. However, the area must be wide enough to give shelter from the wind at ground level. Depending on the site and type of crop the ideal may be anything from 20 m (22 yds) to 60 m (66 yds) in width. A strip 50 m (55 yds) wide and 100 m (110 yds) long is about half a hectare (one acre). The farmer will probably wish to be compensated for the loss of any land devoted to special game crop. This is perfectly reasonable and there are two figures to be considered. Firstly, there is the price for loss of the crop he would have grown on the land concerned, and secondly, the cost of establishing the special game strip. On good arable

(Left) The addition of a strip of cover crop can often turn a hedge or narrow belt into a worthwhile game holding covert.

(Right) Thousand headed kale is more suitable for leaving to go to seed to provide cover for a second year.

ground, a figure of £600 per hectare (£250 per acre) may be realistic. This may seem frightening to the shoot treasurer but if that area results in more birds held on the shoot, better quality presentation or a reduced feed bill, it should be money well spent. It only requires an extra twenty game birds in the bag on most shoots, to justify £250 expenditure. When spending so much money it is vital to ensure that a suitable choice of crop is made and that it is correctly sited. Care and attention over crop husbandry is often critical to successful establishment.

The ability of a crop to provide food, cover, or both, for game is important when deciding on the right plant for a particular site. Obviously in an open downland situation, cover is vital. Equally, alongside a thick hedge or belt, food may be the main requirement to draw birds to the area.

Crops can be divided into three groups - annuals, requiring a full growing season, which will need to be sown in April, May or June (maize, kale and the special mixtures fall into this category); perennials, which also require sowing or planting in April or May, but which, once established, should make fresh growth each year if properly maintained and managed; and catch crops, which are sown after harvest in the hope that sufficient growth may be made by something like mustard to offer a little early season cover.

Kale (*Brassica oleracea*)
Kale is probably the most commonly grown annual crop providing good cover. There is a choice between the marrowstem varieties generally favoured for pheasants because the big flat leaves help in keeping the ground underneath dry, but unsatisfactory in some northern areas because of their susceptibility to frost. Thousand-head varieties which are more frost resistant tend to be wet and offer less protection to birds. The latter are much better at surviving the winter and re-seeding if allowed to go on for a second season. There are some cross-bred varieties such as Maris Kestrel which exhibit some of the more valuable properties of each

57

type; a certain amount of frost hardiness and a reasonably tall stem with some horizontal leaves.

Distance between the drills for a pheasant crop should be greater than the normal 35 cm (14 in.) of a forage crop, with 53 cm (21 in.) being ideal. Sowing can take place from April until June or early July, depending on climate and conditions. Early drilling is advisable in areas where moisture for germination is a problem in the summer, but the young plants may be more susceptible to pigeon damage. A seed rate of 2–4 kilos per hectare (2–4 lbs per acre) is normal when drilling, but this should be doubled for a broadcast crop. The occasional bare area made by deliberately not sowing odd patches can help during driving by providing a place where birds can flush. They also make popular sunning spots in which pheasants can dry out after a spell of wet weather. A straw bale placed in these clearings will be used as a vantage point by both pheasants and partridges.

A very clean crop is seldom as attractive as a weedy one. Fat hen or 'dungweed' is a particular favourite attraction.

A kale and food crop mixture
A development which can improve the drawing ability of a kale strip is to deliberately sow some food crop with it. A simple mixture can be produced by broadcasting a spring cereal and spring field beans (tic-beans) at a third or half their normal agricultural seed rates. This should be harrowed or rotavated in to a suitable depth, after which the kale should be over drilled at its normal seed rate. The grain and beans shed from September to November, while the kale provides the long-term cover late into the season and also gives the important formality of drills.

Other food crops which can be sown with kale to increase its attraction include buckwheat, sunflower, millet, siletina fodder radish, and maize. A weed-free seed bed is required, especially for maize, which is easily stifled by competition.

Mustard (*Brassica alba*)
On poor soils and rough areas such as recently cleared woodland, mustard can prove valuable. It can grow reasonably well with minimum cultivations and on relatively infertile soils. When sown in May or June it should make sufficient

When the cobs ripen in October maize or sweetcorn is one of the most attractive food crops for pheasants.

58

growth to go 'woody' and then stand well into the autumn. However, it does tend to be flattened by snow and for this reason it may be better if the area is drawn into ridges beforehand. This will provide areas in the furrows where birds can find cover and shelter from the wind. A seed rate of 4-6 kilos per hectare (4-6 lbs per acre) should be sufficient.

Food crops

Maize (*Zea mays*)

When the cobs ripen in October maize or sweetcorn is one of the most attractive crops for pheasants. It can draw birds from far and wide, and is often popular with redleg partridges which like the bare floor that it provides. However, this can make it difficult to produce controlled flushes of birds because of the lack of cover at ground level in which they can squat. It also tends to become cold and draughty by Christmas after frost has reduced the leaf and when wind and snow have broken down the stems.

For this reason a strip of maize can be a useful addition alongside a belt of woodland or thick hedge which already gives shelter and provides cover late in the season. An alternative is to establish a block of maize which is surrounded by a cover crop such as kale, mustard, or canary grass. Care must be taken if the atrazine herbicide is used because any drift is likely to kill the shelter crop.

Maize requires a good deal of care and attention to crop husbandry, and ideally needs a special drill so that the seed can be placed 5 cm (2 in.) deep in the ground. It should be sown when the soil temperature is about 4°C (55°F) at 10 cm (4 in.) deep and cannot normally be grown on very high ground or in the harsher British climates.

It often needs special protection against pests, especially during the seedling stage. Mesurol, an anti-frit-fly seed dressing, has some bird repellant qualities but stringing the area with black cotton may be necessary, together with dawn shotgun patrols where crows, rooks, pigeons and pheasants are abundant in the spring. The latter can pose a particular problem because they will walk into the area, ignoring the cottoning.

After Christmas the cover and shelter for game from a food crop such as maize may be drastically reduced by hard weather.

Where the farm grows maize it is sometimes possible to arrange for a strip to be left at the edge of the field in a strategic site for game. Some farmers grow a small field of sweetcorn and pick the cobs for sale until early October, when the remainder is left for pheasants. Initially the birds may have difficulty in finding the food and to help them it is useful to drive a vehicle through or swipe a small patch to bring the cobs down to ground level. Bundles of plants cut and hung in the woods will also be popular with pheasants.

Buckwheat (*Fagopyrum esculentum*)

Buckwheat is a quick-growing polyganum. However, it is not suitable for very northern climates. It matures in 10-12 weeks in the south of England although the seed itself ripens over a longer period. It is attractive to pheasants and partridges, both of which eat the seed.

It is best sown in May after danger of frost has passed at the seed rate of about 40 kilos per hectare (36 lbs per acre) if drilled and 125 kilos per hectare (1 cwt per acre) if broadcast. Its rapid growth is useful in smothering weed competition, but it is flattened by harsh winter weather. Like mustard, it can therefore be valuable to grow it on the ridge. It does not require particularly rich or fertile soils.

Millet (*Panicum effusum*)

The Game Conservancy tried a number of millet varieties in the late 1960's but even in the south they frequently made insufficient growth to give good cover and they did not always ripen. More recently Hungarian varieties have been grown both in mixtures and as pure stands. They have been generally unsuccessful in the north, but reasonable early season cover has been produced in the south of Britain for both pheasants and partridges. By Christmas the cover from a pure crop is no longer sufficient in an exposed position.

However, millet can be grown with the atrazine herbicide and has proved very useful in conjunction with maize. It provides added bottom cover and can improve both shelter and flushing either when drilled in cross bands or broadcast over areas of a maize strip. There are two types: red millet which has a feathery seed head

Fig.13 A block of maize, or maize and millet, surrounded by a cover plant such as kale alongside a suitable hedge is one of the most attractive crops for game, providing both food and shelter.

borne high up on a grassy stalk, and white millet which seems better with its thicker stems and fatter seed heads formed closer to the ground and in range of feeding pheasants and partridges.

A pure stand can be sown in late April or May in 35 cm (14 in.) rows at a seed rate of about 22 kilos per hectare (20 lbs per acre). Because of its susceptibility to being knocked down by hard weather it has been found to be more useful in a mixture or when sheltered by another crop or some permanent cover.

Beans (*Vicia vulgaris*)

Spring field beans, as mentioned, can be an attractive food to pheasants. When grown as a pure crop they seldom stand beyond December except in very sheltered areas, and they can be decimated by pigeons and rooks. However, together with the cereals they are one of the few game food crops that can be grown in the north and on higher ground. They can be particularly useful as the food element in a mixture. Sown on their own, a seed rate of up to 250 kilos per hectare (2 cwts per acre) is normal. This should be reduced to 50-100 kilos per hectare (½ cwt per acre) in mixtures.

Agricultural crops of value to game

It may be that the farm is growing a commercial crop which also provides cover or food for game. In dairy and beef country, big blocks of kale; in sheep areas, large fields of turnips; or in arable parts acres of sugar beet can sometimes be more of a problem than an asset. All these crops can hold large quantities of birds, but with the possible exception of turnips, 4 hectares (10 acres) or more in one block can prove difficult if not impossible to shoot without an armada of dogs and beaters.

Much will depend on how and when the farmer decides to harvest or fold the crop. A strip cut diagonally across a large field may be most helpful because this makes it possible to drive each half to a point. Once cutting or grazing are underway it might be possible to pay for a strategic strip to be left for game, or in the case of sugar beet, be left at least until the early shooting days are over.

Large farm acreages of cover crop can be valuable for holding game but may give problems to the shoot unless they can be cut or grazed into manageable strips.

KIRKLEY HALL

Perennial cover crops

The establishment of relatively small areas of cover crop can be a major agricultural headache each year. This is a particular problem where the ground is prone to kale sickness, and close to woodlands where pests can give frequent trouble. In a difficult site a perennial crop may provide a simple solution.

Artichokes (*Helianthus tuberosus*)
Jerusalem artichokes have been popular as perennial game cover for years. They should be treated like potatoes, being grown from tubers planted on the ridge, but in rows at least 1½ m (4 ft) apart. They must be kept clean and a pre-emergent spray of Round-Up can be the easiest way of weed control. Artichoke tubers are eaten by pheasants late in the season if made available by digging at the side of the ridge, but this cannot be considered a significant draw.

Artichokes make excellent summer cover, and as such can be ideal in an open area of a release pen, but like so many other crops their top growth can be rapidly reduced once the frosts, heavy rain, winds, and snow of winter arrive. One useful technique to help shelter them is the construction of a false hedge from straw bales along their exposed sides. On fertile land they require spinning out, and re-ridging every three or four years. The tubers, incidentally, make excellent soup!

Canary grass (*Phalaris tuberosa*)
This is not to be confused with the annual, canary seed (*Phalaris canariensis*). It is commonly drilled in April or May in 1 m (36–39 in.) wide drills at a seed rate of 5 kilos per hectare (5 lbs per acre) but is unlikely to make sufficient growth to hold game the first year. Whilst establishing, it can be oversown for the first year with mustard, but this makes weed control difficult.

Canary grass is susceptible to very cold winter and spring weather and is therefore not successful at very high altitude or in the north. Crops on north-east facing slopes are particularly vulnerable. The first strip that was sown on Game Conservancy advice some fourteen years ago has been kept clean and correctly managed; it still provides one of the best drives on that particular famous shoot.

Jerusalem artichokes are perennial and once established give good early season cover. Although the tubers are eaten by pheasants they are no substitute for regular feeding with grain.

Catch crops for extra cover

The price that a shoot might realistically be expected to pay for establishment and loss of farm income for an acre of specialist game crop on good arable ground (up to £250) was mentioned earlier. There may also be an opportunity, especially in the warmer climate of the south of Great Britain, to grow a cover crop after the cereal harvest. Naturally, this operation should not eliminate the opportunity of a farm crop for that year, and so compensation for loss of profit is not relevant. Furthermore, the sort of crop that might make sufficient growth in the remainder of the season, once harvest is off, is limited to mustard, fodder radish, and stubble turnip, all of which are relatively cheap and simple to establish.

Of the three, mustard is probably most successful. It germinates quickly, grows fast, and gives reasonable cover until the hard frosts turn it black and knock it flat. Fodder radish is probably marginally slower to germinate, although it grows fast and responds well to a top dressing of nitrogenous fertilizer. Dutch stubble turnips provide poor cover by comparison. They never attain any great height, and consequently tend not to be favoured by pheasants or redleg partridges, although the English bird will frequent them. The leafy growth is inclined to be dense and therefore difficult for gamebirds to run through. They also take a long time to dry after rain or overnight dew.

One most important point to clarify before deciding to drill or broadcast a catch crop is that the area concerned is not destined to be sown in the autumn to a crop like winter barley, wheat, or oil-seed rape. Obviously such an area would be re-cultivated and drilled before the game crop had served any significant purpose.

There is also a very limited growing season in which to establish the catch crop. Generally, if it is not sown by the first week of August, there is little point in bothering. North of a line from the Humber to the Mersey even this date may be too late. Therefore, the best opportunities are after crops like early potatoes, oil-seed rape, or winter barley, which should be harvested by the end of July except in the far north.

Once the field is clear of its agricultural crop no time should be lost. The catch crop seed can be direct drilled straight into the stubble and a pre-emergent spray of Round-Up used to control weeds. (Game Conservancy research has shown that

Canary Grass can give good perennial cover, but planted at 24 in. spacing (as shown here) it rapidly becomes too dense to be attractive to game.

Oversowing mustard into standing corn two or three weeks before harvest can gain precious extra growing time.

Gramoxone is likely to drive birds off stubbles for a few weeks and it can account for a number of hares and rabbits which ingest the toxic chemical when grooming.) Alternatively, the ground may be cultivated before the seed is sown. Four pounds per acre seed rate is adequate for mustard and an applicaton of fertilizer at sowing is also recommended. Then it is a matter of praying for rain to initiate germination. If the attempts fail to produce sufficient growth to make game holding cover, perhaps because of a drought, only a few pounds of seed and fertilizer and a few hours of tractor work have been wasted.

In an attempt to gain a few precious extra weeks growing season some farmers actually 'fiddle' or scatter the mustard into standing corn two or three weeks before harvest. This should be timed before a shower of rain, which should wash the seed into cracks in the ground and initiate germination. After harvest a plant should be established in which case the encouragement of a dose of nitrogenous fertilizer, together with a little moisture, will be all that is necessary to ensure cover up to the top of a wellington boot by late September.

This should at least help hold game in the early part of the season and maybe provide an extra drive or two before the weather turns and frost or snow blackens and flattens the green growth.

6 Broodies

Raising gamebirds under hens or bantams

One of the most fascinating aspects of gamekeeping and running a shoot is observing nature in action. The first attempt at sitting a few picked up pheasant, duck or partridge eggs from a deserted nest under a bantam, if successful, can be very rewarding.

As already mentioned, there are many practical reasons why the small and part-time 'keepered shoot should think carefully before embarking on a full-scale mechanical incubation operation. The most obvious is the problem posed by seven or eight different hatch dates of day-olds which will then require rearing and, if pheasants, releasing in separate batches and in different pens. The second is the cost in terms of equipment and time to carry out the various incubation stages successfully.

Where only a few birds, perhaps less than a hundred, are to be raised, the broody hen has many advantages. If nests in foolish sites are frequently found or the local farm staff and verge cutters are looking out for endangered clutches, it pays to keep some broodies ready to receive hot eggs - that is, eggs which have already been incubated for a period and in which the embryo has started to develop. Some 'keepers deliberately reduce the number of eggs in the wild grey partridge's nest down to ten or possibly twelve, on the grounds that under modern conditions, the pair is more likely to rear a small family of chicks to maturity than a large brood of fifteen or more. This will release the surplus eggs for hatching and rearing and the broody bantam is a particularly well proven method of raising 'the Englishman'.

Keeping a stock of sitters

Sadly, the stock of potential broodies is no longer sufficient in many areas of Britain to be able to buy or borrow when required. Gone are the times when 'keepers could collect enough steady hens on a morning round the local small-holdings to raise several hundred pheasants. These days it is safer to keep your own fowl of suitable breeding. Years ago the Game Conservancy took great trouble to establish the good and the not so successful breeds of poultry for incubating and rearing game. Ignoring the detail, the basic rules are: - avoid modern egg-laying strains which have had the broody instinct carefully bred out of them; the old-fashioned breeds are much preferred and game fowl and silkies have consistently proved good mothers. For duck, a large hen is required to cover a quantity of eggs, while for partridge eggs, a smaller bantam is needed if the clutch is not to be squashed under heavy, clumsy feet. Crosses tend to be steadier sitters than the pure breeds, and it pays, in the first instance, to buy from someone who has used their stock as 'clockers'.

The 'good life' fraternity are inclined to keep their hens and bantams on such a free range basis that the nests can never be found and therefore neither can the broodies, especially when they are most wanted. It is easier if the stock is penned and have to use the laying boxes provided. In this way a close eye can be kept on their behaviour. Also by darkening off the sitting boxes, baiting the nests with dummies and increasing the plane of nutrition, broodiness can sometimes be induced when required.

Amateurs occasionally introduce a clutch of gamebird eggs straight under a hen in the laying box when a particular fowl is considered to have 'gone down' for a suitable period. Occasionally the exception proves the rule and some eggs hatch. To be more certain of success the correct equipment, a proper sitting box, carefully sited, is necessary to provide the right sort of managed environment for the eggs to develop and hatch into healthy chicks.

Hatching under broodies

A steady broody is an asset almost beyond value to the old-fashioned game rearer. Once established as a successful foster mother the same hen or bantam is inclined to perform as desired each year. But it always pays to be sure, and therefore it is as well to set up the sitting boxes with some dummy eggs so that any fowl thought to be broody can be given a few test days before introducing the real thing.

Nest boxes normally measure about 40 cm (16 in.) square and are built in batteries. Alternatively, a coop can be used. Either should be sited in a sheltered and shaded place such as under trees, shrubs, or on the northern side of a wall. A saucer-shaped nest should be made in the earth, taking care to remove any stones from the ground. During incubation these are inclined to rise to the surface and cause eggs to crack. Long grass is ideal to make a nest lining.

Where only a few birds are to be raised, hatching and rearing under the broody hen has many advantages.

66

Where silage or hay are made, gamebird nests will inevitably be destroyed. It pays to keep some broodies on dummies ready to receive 'hot' eggs.

The hen or bantam should be taken out of the box to feed and water at approximately the same time every day, normally in the morning. A stick with a length of tethering string is required to secure the fowl by one leg so that it may walk about, do its droppings, feed and water, but not vanish without trace. After a few days of such handling whilst on dummies, the hen should be sufficiently steady to introduce a clutch of real eggs. In the first week of incubation, the hen should not be allowed off for more than seven minutes. This is because the developing embryo is very small and therefore most vulnerable to chilling. During the second week, ten to twelve minutes should be safe whilst twenty minutes can be permitted in warm weather afterwards.

In a dry period, or if the sitting boxes are sited in an arid position, it pays to sprinkle a little warm water on the eggs from the twenty-first day until the clutches hatch. This should be done just before the hen or bantam is being returned to the eggs.

Fig.14 Broodies in sitting boxes should be tended at about the same time each day by tethering within range of feed and water.

Once the chicks have hatched, provided the fowl is not clumsy with her feet, there is no need to rush the family out into the open. The young will benefit from twelve to twenty-four hours brooding and they will still be receiving nourishment from reserves retained in their yolk sacs.

Introducing chicks to a broody

Sometimes hens and bantams are kept on dummy eggs with the intention of using them just to rear chicks and possibly to help with release, but not for incubation. If this is the case they should have been sitting for at least a week and preferably longer before an attempt is made to present the 'clocker' with the chicks.

It is best to introduce them at night, taking care to minimise disturbance to the hen. She should be in a dark laying box and observed carefully for long enough to be reasonably certain that she will not reject her adopted brood. Pecking at the chicks' heads or flightiness are symptoms of rejection, in which case another hen should be tried. It therefore pays to have spare broodies that have been sitting for a while. After a night in a dark laying box the hen and chicks can be moved to a coop and run for the rearing stage.

A coop with corrugated iron sheets attached to each side and one end-piece can make an adequate movable unit for broody rearing.

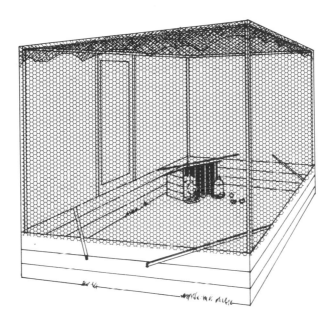

Fig.15 A 3 m x 1.5 m (10 ft x 6 ft) movable pen, with the broody confined initially to a coop. The chickfood and drinker are placed within range of the hen.

Rearing with broodies

A coop with a sheet of corrugated iron attached to each side and joined with an end piece makes an adequate unit for rearing. The hen will normally be confined to the coop but able to share the special game chick crumb food and the drink by stretching head and neck through the slatted front. The chicks will have access to the run although some 'keepers prefer to limit the area available to them in the first few days. Even if a movable pen is used and a coop placed inside it, the option is available to give the brood fresh ground whenever desirable. This action, together with providing food and water and ensuring that predators are denied access to the run, is all the work that is required. No heaters, de-beaking, bitting, worries about pile-ups and suffocation are involved. Even shutting in at night may be unnecessary.

7 Brooder Rearing

Is restocking necessary?

Especially in the drier, predominantly arable areas of Britain there are many shoots which produce excellent results by managing the natural stock, with no releasing at all. Often when reared birds have been marked on shoots in such parts the recovery rates have revealed that the time and effort involved in their production and release would have been much more effectively devoted to encouraging the wild birds.

There is also some evidence, from observation, to suggest that released pheasants (especially in the first season after release) are not such good mothers as their wild cousins. The Game Conservancy are currently engaged in a research project to investigate this contention, which clearly has important implications for restocking in areas potentially good for natural production.

To rear or buy in?

Where releasing is required to ensure there is some game on the ground, it may still be unwise to rear one's own birds. Capital cost is involved in buying the necessary equipment, which might be more usefully spent on other aspects. Rearing, even on the back lawn, demands a regular daily commitment for at least a six-week period and for the initial stages several inspections each day are necessary.

The actual rearing operations are in no way complicated. Anyone with some idea about animals and a little common sense can raise a high proportion of day-old chicks into tough well-feathered poults. However, if only a hundred or two birds are involved there is a good argument to leave this job to the specialists, the gamefarmers, and buy in poults. This will release valuable time which can be devoted to tending to the wild stock and preparing for the arrival of the reared birds.

A conventional brooder unit

When the Game Conservancy began pheasant rearing trials in little huts with electric heaters some thirty years ago, many shooting folk and gamekeepers remarked that the tests were a waste of time. If poults could be produced by such a system 'they would never survive, and gamebirds must be reared under broodies for release into the wild', was the generally accepted response.

From those original pioneering experiments have developed today's 150 or so gamefarms and the tens of thousands of shoots which use brooder rearing to produce birds for re-stocking. A number of different systems have evolved, but they are mostly adaptations and scale variations of the original 'Fordingbridge Unit' which was designed to produce 100 pheasant poults.

The Unit consists of a portable hut made from exterior ply which measures 1.5 m by 1.5 m (5 ft x 5 ft) with a sloping roof about 1.4 m (4 ft 6 in.) tall. Ventilation is given through a series of holes drilled close to the roof on two of the sides, but to prevent wind causing a draught these are covered with a plank set out as a baffle. Light and a way of increasing ventilation is provided by a window of wire netting about 0.5 m (18 in.) square in the front, which has a sliding plywood cover. The door itself is of the stable type so that chicks do not pour out every time it is opened. At least two corners are fitted with popholes, one of which gives access to the next chamber, the nursery run.

The sooner chicks are allowed out of the hut the quicker they begin to acclimatise to natural conditions, but obviously for the first weeks of life they are vulnerable to cold and wet weather. A nursery pen, an area protected from the rain, allows young birds to be gradually exposed to outside conditions. Two 3 m (10 ft) sections leant together and covered with clear polythene, but with the triangular ends covered with only netting to give ventilation, are adequate for a 100 bird unit.

Finally the nursery pen, which can double as a night shelter later in the rearing process, is connected by a pophole to an outside run made from portable pen sections. An area 6 m (20 ft) square, covered with a small mesh soft roof net to exclude starlings and sparrows is sufficient, but young pheasants in particular will enjoy more space. Half an old motor car tyre nailed to a pole makes a suitable prop to hold up the net. The grass in the outside run can be allowed to grow tall, provided tracks are cut through it at the edge. A central mown area is the ideal place to locate feeders and drinkers. As an alternative the outside run can be made from sections 3 m (10 ft) or so tall which are leant together to form an arch. This

Fig.16 The modern rearing unit comprises a brooder hut, a nursery pen with covered top, and an outside run with roof net.

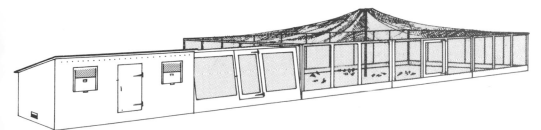

has a number of advantages: there is no need for a roof net; there may be no need for a nursery pen if some sections are given extra cladding on the sides to give shelter to the chicks in inclement weather; and it is much easier to drive young birds into the brooder house with the long narrow-shaped run. However, this system is generally more expensive in terms of initial purchase.

The brooder hut can be heated by calor gas or electrcity, depending on availability and preference. It must be remembered that mains electricity is subject to power cuts, especially in areas where summer thunder storms are common. The bedding material most commonly used in a hut with no floor is pea gravel, which drains well and retains heat. Alternatively, untreated hardwood shavings make excellent bedding, particularly on a hard floor. There is a risk that some chicks may eat shavings and to avoid this they can be covered with corrugated cardboard or hessian for a few days.

Corners should be blanked off with triangular tin, wood or hardboard inserts. Young gamebird chicks can be remarkably stupid to the extent of becoming disorientated and lost in a corner, while with larger units 'pile-ups' resulting in some suffocations can occur.

There are many different sizes of unit now available and most are developments of the basic Fordingbridge design. 250-bird brooder systems are probably more common today. These are likely to comprise a hut of 2.4 m by 2 m (8 ft by 6 ft), a shelter pen of 3 m (10 ft) square, with an outer run measuring 10 m (30 ft) square. Even larger units suitable for taking up to 500 chicks are available with brooder houses resembling garden sheds.

The Rupert brooder

The Rupert is of a very different design to the conventional unit. It consists of a low, circular, tin 'hut' which is heated by paraffin or calor gas. The heat and fumes are carried through a series of pipes along the ceiling. Temperature is controlled by turning the burners up or down, these being situated in a separate compartment.

An insulating cover is available to prevent the direct rays of the sun over-heating the unit. This also cuts out the danger of chicks being driven out of the brooder

To avoid the risk of chicks eating shavings used as bedding, the shavings can be covered with corrugated cardboard for the first few days. Food and drink should be visible but shaded.

72

by the din of heavy rain or hail on the tin roof. There is no other cover or shelter provided other than by the brooder and the surrounding sections. It therefore tends to produce tough poults and is considered by some to be particularly suitable for rearing birds destined for release into the harsher climates of the north. The Hardwick brooder is similar in looks and concept and is also available in a larger size. The common criticism of such designs is that they are difficult to see into and require a great deal of hands and knees activity. This can become tiresome if large numbers of birds are involved.

Brooder rearing routine

Rearing hardy chicks in most brooder systems is relatively easy, but it is a good procedure to assume that the chicks really wish to commit suicide and therefore every precaution and measure must be taken to ensure that they have no opportunity to do so.

If chicks are being obtained from a gamefarm it is useful to know exactly when they were hatched. If they have been taken straight from the incubator it may pay to leave them boxed in a room of even temperature for a few hours. They will be living on the remains of the yolk sac and gaining strength at this stage. At least 48 hours before the chicks are due the brooder house should be prepared and the heater made operational to warm up the chicks' intended accommodation. Hopefully, any defects such as blown fuses, faulty elements or blocked gas jets will reveal themselves at this stage before the young birds are at risk.

The temperature at ground level in the hut should be between 31 and 32°C (90 and 95° F) to start, but once in residence, the chicks themselves are the best indicators. When they are huddled together under the heater they are too cold and the lamp should be lowered; equally, if they are spread far away from the direct warmth, they are too hot and the brooder should be raised by shortening the chain.

For the first few days a circle of cardboard or hardboard should be installed to limit the area available to that under the heater and the near surroundings. Food and water should be placed where they can easily be seen, preferably in a light spot not directly under the brooder. Reducing the illumination in a brooder house has a definite calming effect on the chicks and can help to reduce feather picking, but

The Rupert Brooder tends to produce tough chicks. There is only the brooder and canopy for shelter.

73

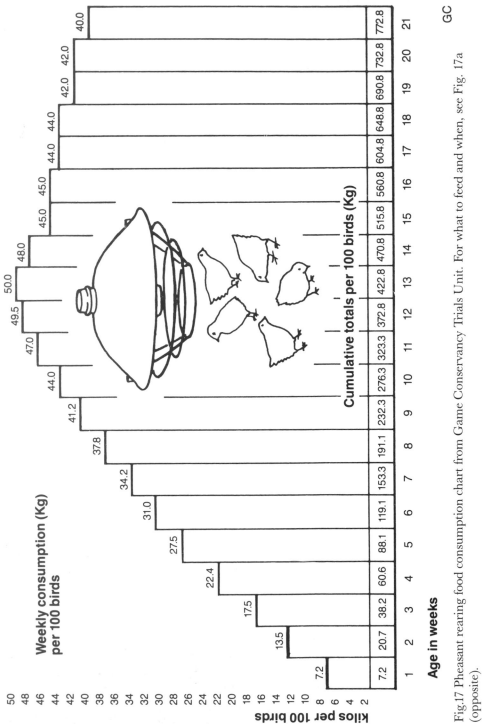

Weekly consumption (Kg) per 100 birds

7.2	13.5	17.5	22.4	27.5	31.0	34.2	37.8	41.2	44.0	47.0	49.5	50.0	48.0	45.0	45.0	44.0	44.0	42.0	42.0	40.0

kilos per 100 birds

50 48 46 44 42 40 38 36 34 32 30 28 26 24 22 20 18 16 14 12 10 8 6 4 2

Cumulative totals per 100 birds (Kg)

7.2	20.7	38.2	60.6	88.1	119.1	153.3	191.1	232.3	276.3	323.3	372.8	422.8	470.8	515.8	560.8	604.8	648.8	690.8	732.8	772.8
1	2	3	4	5	6	7	8	9	10	11	12	13	14	15	16	17	18	19	20	21

Age in weeks

GC

Fig.17 Pheasant rearing food consumption chart from Game Conservancy Trials Unit. For what to feed and when, see Fig. 17a (opposite).

74

—————— Super Chick Crumbs:
first 2-3 weeks especially with intensively reared stock

— — — —————— Pheasant Chick Crumbs: up to 5-6 weeks

— — — —————— Pheasant Chick Pellets:
from 3-5 weeks depending on bitting and familiarisation needs

—————— Pheasant Rearing Pellets:
a good acclimatising ration; a little grain if desired

————————————— Pheasant Growing Pellet:
with increasing use of grain

—————————————

1 2 3 4 5 6 7 8 9 10 11 12   age in weeks

Fig.17a What to feed and when: lines and dashes indicate recommended periods. (See Fig. 17).

Temperature is normally controlled by raising or lowering the lamp, with the chicks' behaviour being the best indicator. Note that initially the chicks are restricted by a cardboard circle to the vicinity of the heater.

The Game Conservancy Letterbox feeder attachment with a drum makes an inexpensive weatherproof hopper for the outside run.

at first there must be sufficient light for the birds to find food and water. Chick crumbs can be fed on papier-maché egg keys trays which are convenient, cheap and therefore disposable. This means that new ones can be introduced frequently. Special jam jar chick drinkers are available from most game and poultry equipment suppliers but at first a few pebbles should be placed in the trough to prevent any possibility of chicks drowning.

In warm weather, the window can be opened to increase ventilation. It must be remembered that temperatures can fall dramtically at night, and therefore these windows may require closing each evening in the early stages and it may be necessary to lower the brooder to increase the heat.

At any stage between a few days old and three weeks the young birds may be given access to the nursery pen by opening the pophole but to begin with only a small area should be made available if the chicks are still very small. The grass in this area should be mown short because until quills and feathers grow (from two weeks old and onwards) the covering of fluff can be drenched by long moist vegetation, destroying its insulating properties.

From about the third week the chick crumbs can be gradually replaced by a mini-pellet of slightly lower protein content, and by this stage proper poultry troughs or Game Conservancy letterbox feeders should have been substituted for the keys trays.

Depending on personal preference, the weather and the species being reared, the young poults may be given access to the outer run at any stage from ten days to four weeks of age. If birds are allowed out at an early age, which should help to encourage good 'hardening off', they should be quietly chased back into the safety of the nursery pen every evening, hence the alternative name for this covered area of night shelter.

By four weeks a full-sized pheasant pellet should be introduced and unless conditions are particularly inclement the heater in the brooder house can be switched off permanently. Obviously it is then possible to separate the brooder hut and after thorough cleansing, set it up to take another batch of chicks.

Game rearing in buildings

On many shoots the raw materials for making a rearing unit already exist in some form. A little conversion or adaptation can make many a building, shed or even caravan into suitable quarters for game production. A stable or loose-box can double as a brooder house.

Care should be taken to ensure that there is suitable ventilation without draughts. It may be necessary to install a false ceiling to prevent excessive heat loss. This can be done very simply with polythene sheet and some battens. A floor area in the region of 4 m (12 ft) square is adequate space to rear 350 to 400 pheasants up to the three-week stage in comfort, providing it is possible to give the chicks access via a pophole to a nursery pen and to an outside run. An alternative is to rear the chicks up to three or four weeks old inside and when they are 'off heat' to move them to an open grass run with a shelter pen so that they have at least two to three weeks 'hardening off' before release.

Garages and old piggeries are often successfully adapted to rear gamebirds but sometimes the outside run is omitted. 'Hardening off' is then totally artificial because the birds have no exposure to the outside, the elements, or grass until they are shifted to the release pens at about seven weeks old. Instead, they are sprayed briefly with a mist of water droplets. A knapsack sprayer is ideal for the purpose, which is to wet the birds but not to soak the bedding and inside of the building. This system is simpler if there is a small outside area because then a garden hose with a nozzle producing a fine spray can be used, and the water can drain away. It is helpful to provide some low 'roosting' poles. The young birds will hop up on these and begin to preen their wet feathers. The purpose of this activity is to use the oil secreted by the gland at the base of the tail and spread it through the feathers. It can be regarded as the gamebirds' system of water-proofing its coat, which is obviously vital before it is exposed to the rain.

There can be no doubt that birds reared in these relatively intensive systems can and will survive release. A shoot close to Fordingbridge has been restocking with poults, which are reared in a shed with small concrete outside runs, but they are artificially 'hardened off' by the sprinkling system described. For a number of seasons, recovery rates of tagged birds have exceeded the national average of 40%,

A quick spray on hot days and the provision of 'roosting' poles is a useful way of 'hardening off' birds in intensive units.

and on occasions have been approaching 60%, which is remarkable on a shoot where the main covert days and two-thirds of the birds are shot in January. There can be no doubt that intensively reared poults are acclimatising successfully to the wild in this case.

For redleg partridges, chukars, and the cross or ogridge, the converted building can make an excellent rearing unit. Often these birds are not released until 10 or even 12 weeks old and so they may be held inside for longer and the 'hardening off' stage delayed for a period. Many gamefarmers and 'keepers find them easier to rear than pheasants. Because they tend to be quite docile in captivity, they are especially suitable for intensive rearing.

The standard of management of any intensive units must be especially good. With 500 or more birds in a batch confined to relatively close quarters, the risk of trouble or disease is that much greater and if disaster strikes the losses can be tremendous. Hygiene must be meticulous with all equipment kept constantly clean, and approved poultry disinfectants used. Fortunately, brick, breeze block, and concrete are all relatively easy to wash. If the birds look ill in any way or if losses are greater than can reasonably be expected, do not hesitate to collect three or more corpses together and take them for immediate post-mortem. Luckily, most ailments are curable in the rearing unit, but deaths can occur in horrifying numbers from a wide variety of diseases and therefore it is wise to be safe rather than sorry and investigate any sign of trouble so that it can be nipped in the bud.

Feather picking

The main problem for amateur and professional pheasant rearer alike is that of feather picking. It is not a vice restricted to gamebirds, the poultry industry has been burdened with it for decades, but fortunately it is much less common in grey and redleg partridges.

In the pheasant, feather picking can start at any time after a few days old, but it is most prevalent from three weeks until the release stage. Numerous reasons

Fig.18 The split of a bit clips into the nostrils of the bird so that the ring prevents the beak from closing completely. The bird can still feed freely from a trough.

have been advanced as to its causes by gamekeepers, poulterers, and research scientists. The intensification of the rearing process from the natural operation leads to a stress factor due to density. It is also considered that pheasants provided with sheds, shelters, runs, food and water become bored and aggression expressed in feather picking is one result. The other significant theory is that nutritional deficiency is partly to blame and that a desire for amino acids, such as arganine contained in feathers, is a possible reason for pheasants to start pecking. Sadly, the real cause and therefore a foolproof preventative have not yet been discovered. Instead, mechanical aids which stop the damage normally caused by the pecking are frequently used.

The traditional system of preventing damage is to clip the tip of the top mandible (the upper half of the beak). This stops a bird from actually holding the feather of another bird securely enough to pull it out. Damage can be inflicted if the upper beak is trimmed too severely, and it is important not to cut back beyond the transluscent creamy section into the blueish area which contains the blood supply. Provided the cutting is careful the operation should not be any more serious than trimming toe nails. If only a few poults are involved then a pair of tough scissors, nail clippers, or electrical snips are adequate, but for a large number of birds it pays to invest in an electric de-beaker which will actually singe the tip of the upper mandible and cauterize at the same time.

The alternative is to use a 'bit' - a plastic or metal ring with a split in it. The split should be inserted into the nares, the nostrils of the bird, while the ring fits between the upper and lower beak so it cannot completely shut. Again this prevents a bird from holding a feather sufficiently securely to pull it out of another bird. Bits come in three different sizes: A - small, for one to three weeks old, B - medium, for three to six or seven weeks old, and C - large for adult birds. The plastic model is simple to put in and remove by hand, but occasionally a few can fall out. Thus for a large batch of pheasants the alloy bits, which are pinched into place with a pair of pliers and should be snipped out before release, are often preferred. It is a nightmare job trying to find the 20 or so poults that have lost their plastic bits out of a unit of 500!

An electric debeaker (powered by a car battery) will actually singe the tip of the upper mandible and cauterise at the same time.

The most common age for poults to peck is from three weeks old until release, therefore the size B is the normal bit used. It is absolutely vital that all bits of whatever size are removed from birds before they are released into the wild. If feather picking or tail pecking is anticipated in the release pen it may be a wise precaution to administer a light de-beaking and the effects of this should give some protection for ten days or more.

These mechanical methods are most effective at stopping birds from damaging each other but do not impair their ability to eat or drink, providing food is supplied in troughs. The action of catching up of pheasants to apply the precaution is itself likely to cause extra stress. Therefore the ideal is where no such precaution is necessary. Plenty of space, an abundance of cover, extra greenstuffs, minimum disturbance, chicks of uniform colour, and careful considerate management will sometimes prevent feather picking problems arising. However, if any sign of trouble is seen, quick action is necessary to limit the effects of this highly contagious vice.

Redleg partridges

There are two rearing troubles commonly encountered when rearing redlegged partridges. Toe pecking can break out at any stage during the first week or so, and it can spread rapidly, if not checked, until eventually it may lead to cannibalism. Using shavings as bedding tends to reduce the likelihood of an outbreak, possibly because the shiny toenails of the birds are partly hidden in the litter. If trouble starts it can be contained by a light de-beaking.

The other all too familiar ailment which afflicts young redlegs is coccidiosis. The disease is species specific. That is to say, a form which affects pheasants will not trouble redlegs. However, redlegs are prone to attack by some very virulent strains which tend to occur between the three-week and release stage. A light outbreak cured by the recommended water soluble treatment of Amprol-Plus can be a blessing in disguise. Once birds have been affected they normally build up a natural immunity against further attacks.

Grey partridges

Grey partridges are considered by most 'keepers to be more difficult to rear than pheasants or redlegs. The young chicks require a higher plane of nutrition and therefore some gamefood manufacturers market a special partridge super-starter crumb of up to 31% protein content. It should only be used for the first two weeks or so otherwise there is some danger of the birds going off their feet. This is said to be caused by the body out-growing the bones. It appears only to give trouble in larger units where rearing is performed in huts or indoors and there is no access to the outside and grass.

Mallard are relatively easy to rear, but they use a considerable quantity of water.

Another alarming phenomenon sometimes exhibited by grey partridges in brooder rearing units is a form of hysteria. Outbreaks usually occur from six weeks old onwards and often in hot dry weather. Sprinkling with a mist of water, cooling them down, can be of temporary help, but ultimately the only solution appears to be to split the birds into much smaller units, even down to a large covey size of 25 or so.

Mallard

Duck are among the easiest of all birds to rear. In fact, the management has to be seriously at fault for real trouble to occur unless there is an unfortunate outbreak of disease. It is wise to rear them separately from game because they can carry a number of ailments which may prove fatal to pheasants or partridges. Obviously, treatments of a mechanical nature such as de-beaking or bitting are not possible for mallard.

Perhaps there should be one word of warning. Ducklings need a tremendous quantity of water and often use a substantial amount of it to create an appalling muddy mess! Therefore plenty of space or even better, a movable outer run, is advisable.

8 Releasing Pheasants

Siting release pens

The perfect site for a pheasant release pen to stock an area is determined by a wide range of different factors. One of the great fascinations of game management is that no two shoots are the same but certain obvious principles can be applied when making the choice of where to construct pens.

The traditional custom of releasing pheasants in woods where birds are wanted for a particular drive later in the season have now been superseded by a more logical system. In the modern theory the release pen is regarded as a home base for the pheasant and a target area to which it should fly when flushed from nearby coverts. The less the bird is disturbed by driving and shooting in this home base, the greater the chance of it being content to remain within range of the pen. Therefore a wood which is central to a number of good drives, but which is not necessarily of any great merit as a drive in itself, is ideal.

For the do-it-yourself 'keepering situation where time may be the most limiting factor, geographical considerations may become secondary to ease of access for servicing. Pheasants should be fed at least twice a day at release, and dogging poults into the pen each evening is important in the early stages. Therefore a pen which is several fields away from farm tracks or woodland rides may be totally impractical. The situation can be further aggravated if water has to be carried in by hand.

In direct conflict with accessibility for the 'keeper is the vulnerability of a release pen to poachers. Large-scale poaching operations can wreck a restocking programme, and ease of removal of the bounty is an important feature to the thieves. Consequently, siting pens near public areas or farm tracks can be risky unless a trusted person lives close-by or a detection system is in use.

The other vital consideration is that suitable habitat is available for the young poults to acclimatise to the wild. The three most important constituents of the release pen are open sunny areas, good ground vegetation giving both shelter and escape cover, and sufficient bushes or young trees with horizontal branches to provide low roosting. Releasing pheasants into crops or other areas without roosting facilities generally gives poor returns, except in special circumstances such as the complete absence of foxes and other large ground predators. The sunny and shrub areas should be evenly distributed. Large open patches can leave poults vulnerable to birds of prey, while very dense thickets may be impenetrable to young pheasants.

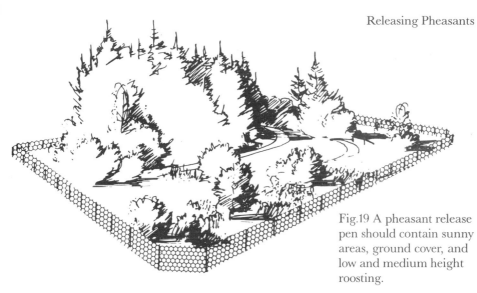

Fig.19 A pheasant release pen should contain sunny areas, ground cover, and low and medium height roosting.

If a site with light soil can be chosen, the birds may be less liable to outbreaks of disease. Very alkali or very acid ground is also useful in limiting the opportunity for gapes. The alternate hosts of the disease, invertebrates such as slugs and worms, thrive on neutral soils. This explains the old-fashioned 'keepers' treatment of liming the ground but it should be remembered that this is only effective where the pH is above 7.

The treatment of many of the common pheasant diseases involves water soluble products. Therefore while natural water by way of ponds and streams in a pen can cut out the burden of carting drink to the poults, it can also prove positively infuriating if the young birds will not take their medicine because they prefer the natural water supply.

Sufficient bushes or young trees with low branches are important to encourage poults to start roosting.

All these factors, together with special local conditions, should be considered very carefully before deciding on how many release pens are required and the precise positions to start their construction. A 'permanent' pen should last ten years before the wire needs replacing and several hours and probably days of hard work will be devoted to its building, therefore it pays to be right first time.

Constructing a pheasant release pen

The most popular system of liberating and acclimatising young pheasant poults to the wild in the British Isles is through open-topped pens. By clipping the outer feathers of one wing a seven-week-old bird should remain in the safety of the release area for a period of about three weeks. The considerable expense and difficulties of roof netting are avoided and larger pens can be made with sufficient roosting trees included.

Fig.20 Release pen construction.
(a) The simplest way to start is by cutting a track along which to mount the fence.
(b) The netting should run to 6 ft high at least, with an anti-predator fringe top and bottom.
(c) Sharp corners should be avoided.

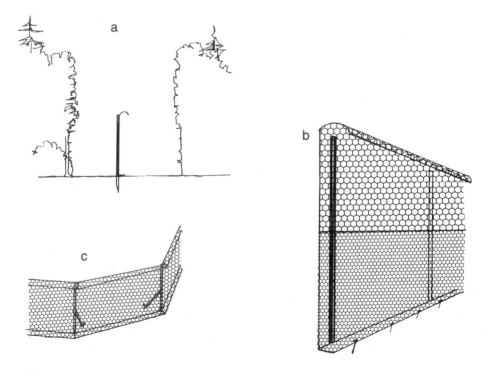

Having identified the most suitable site, the area that should be enclosed can be marked. Often the simplest way of starting is to cut a track through existing wood and shrub cover of 5 to 10m (5–11 yds) in width along which the perimeter fence will be erected. Of course, the occasional straight stemmed and brashed tree can be left if these are to be used as posts. Wire netting should be tied with plastic twine on to live trees and never nailed or stapled. Not only does ironmongery ruin the tree for commercial purposes and possibly also damage saws at felling time, but expansion during growth will often stretch the wire to breaking point.

Posts can often be cut from nearby in the wood, but even chestnut and larch have a relatively short life span if they are not properly preserved. Tannalised timbers appear to last longer than other treatments, but if posts are to be purchased it may pay to invest in metal T-bar or angle iron. This is much easier to drive into hard ground and should last longer than any treated wood. A lick of rustproof paint is worthwhile otherwise corrosion can spread from the iron to start premature decay in the galvanised netting.

Wire netting should be at least 2 m (6 ft) high, but on sloping ground it may need to be much taller to prevent larger mammalian predators jumping it. Most 'keepers prefer to use a small mesh of up to 38 mm (1½ in.) on the bottom while the top half can be up to 75 mm (3 in.) because its main purpose is to stop birds flying out. Care should be taken to ensure all joins in the wire netting are entirely secure. At least 25 cm (10 in.) should be dug in or laid out and pegged at the base with 40 cm (15in.) or so folded out at the top to form an anti-predator fringe. Sharp corners should be avoided with anything tighter than a right-angle being undesirable. If the initial track has been cleared as suggested there should be little extra tree pruning required to ensure no outhanging or inhanging branches. The former encourage birds to fly off roost on the outside of the wire, while the latter can act as a ladder giving easy access for predators which can climb. The wire netting itself should be floppy to prevent its use as a potential climbing frame.

Doors must be as secure as the rest of the pen. It is astonishing how often when Game Conservancy consultants have been called to comment after a break in and big kill in a release pen that the offending predator has made its entry through a poorly made door. It may pay to have several doors, and in large pens it can be useful to make a small door within a large portable section which can be removed to give vehicle access for carting food, water, brush-cutting implements, and even the poults themselves. Of course, at some stage during the season beaters may require to blank the pen out, and therefore many doors will be essential unless provision has been made to lift certain sections of the netting at the base when the poults are satisfactorily acclimatised.

Provision must be made for the young pheasants to walk back into the pen once their primary feathers have grown and they make their first flights out. Sadly, few birds will have the sense to fly back to the safety of the pen each evening. Every 50 m (55 yds) or so 'lead-in wings' are required to direct pheasants into a re-entry

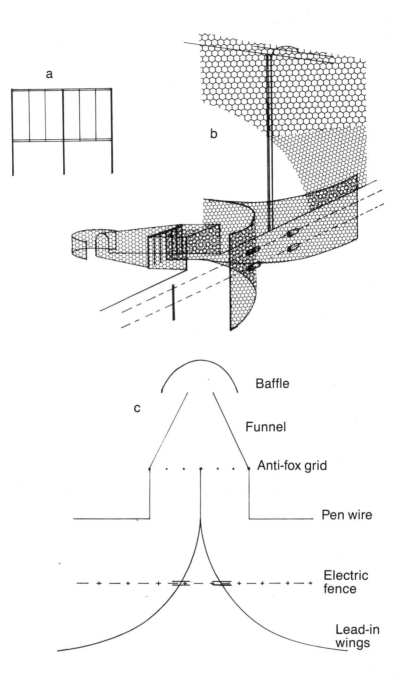

Fig.21 Release pen construction.
(a) Game Conservancy anti-fox grid;
(b) re-entry funnel with non-exit baffle, lead-in wings and electric fence positions;
(c) an aerial view of the funnel.

funnel. This should be fitted with an anti-predator grid made of steel and of suitable dimensions to allow pheasants to pass through up to twelve weeks old while denying access to a fox. A gap of 9 cm (3½ in.) between the uprights will allow poults up to this age to squeeze through while preventing a normal adult fox. However, at release time cubs may be about so it will pay to blank off the grids with wire netting until the first few birds have been seen going 'over the top'.

Preparing a pheasant release pen

Release pens should always be checked well before pheasants are due for release. It is astonishing how much dilapidation can occur from one year to the next, especially if the pen area is enclosing part of a drive and the wire netting has been lifted. This action seems to accelerate rot and the rate at which holes appear.

The next step will be to mow or cut a ride through the vegetation around the inside and outside of the pen wire. A tractor mounted swipe or jungle-buster is ideal for this purpose on large pens where there is easy access. If there are very large impenetrable clumps of thick cover within the pen it may pay to bash out some tracks so that young poults can meander through such thickets rather than be excluded from them. Also feed rides and sunning areas will need to be cleared and shelters checked or rebuilt.

Once the annual herbaceous growth has been adequately opened up it will be easier to make a detailed inspection to check that the wire is still sound. Hopefully, any lower wire netting which has been lifted will have been pegged back down in late winter or the spring to allow grass and weeds to grow through the meshes, thus helping to secure the lower anti-predator fringe.

Where foxes exist or domestic pets are known to stray, an electric fence is a very necessary deterrent. Ideally, two strands, the first 15 cm (6 in.) and the second 30 cm (1 ft) off the ground, should be erected to surround the pen. Views on the best distance from the pen wire vary but the Game Conservancy suggest from 40 cm (15 in.) to 50 cm (20in.) Where the fence passes through the 'lead in wings' of the re-entry funnels the wires should be passed through rubber hosepipe for insulation. Care must be taken to ensure no vegetation grows up to cause a short, and a spray of weedkiller such as Gramoxone, Round-Up, or Pre-fix granules several weeks before the birds are due should ensure this. A removable insulated join should be made where doors open out to avoid fouling the electric wires. Once installed, most electric fence units can be heard to be operational by their ticking noise. However, a mere blade of grass growing up to touch the wire can short the circuit, and that is sufficient to allow a determined predator to make its entry. It is astonishing how often just one night's failure is all that is required for a fox to capitalise on the situation, and create carnage on the unfortunate inhabitants of the pen. The wire and insulators are relatively cheap although the power unit may cost in the region

Some protection against the nocturnal human intruders to release pens can be given by cheap and simple alarm mines. They are normally triggered by anglers' monofil set across tracks or rides at suitable height and are armed with Eley black powder saluting blanks.

of £60. As a means of insuring against the entry of large ground predators to the pen it should soon repay for its investment. Alternatively it may be possible to borrow a unit from a local stock farmer for the most critical period, which is the first six weeks after the poults have been released.

Other tricks and devices to dissuade potential poult predators may also be used. Many 'keepers like to hang up sacking soaked in diesel as a further fox deterrent, while flashing lights may dissuade brown owls, glitter-bangs can scare sparrow hawks, and even radios or tape recorders as a pretence of human presence can be useful additions.

On many shoots it has become necessary to install some sort of protection from the human predator. Whether it be simple alarm mines, trip guns, or a more sophisticated poacher detector system, the installation should be given a pre-season test to ensure that it is fully operational and ready for action.

Birds to wood

Fierce debate frequently rages over the ideal time of year to release pheasants. Some gamekeepers argue that early birds do best, while others explain that late birds may hold better because they have less time before the season starts in which to wander. Game Conservancy research over several decades indicates that the mid-period pheasants released in late July and early August tend to give the best returns.

Of course every shoot is different. Where cover is sparse and liable to be laid low by frost or snow, early birds with the main shoots in November/December may be sensible. Equally, on ground with large woodland where ride shooting is predominant, later poults can be acceptable because the season cannot commence in earnest until the leaf is off, often the third week in November.

The age at which pheasants are released is dictated mainly by the open-top pen system used by most shoots. The primary flight feathers of the young pheasant moult from the inside outward and at between six and seven weeks of age about four to six of the outermost feathers of one wing can be clipped. Over the next two to three weeks the remaining stubs will be cast and new adult flights will grow to replace them. This gives a vital period for the poults to acclimatise to the wild and

At about six to seven weeks old the *outer* 5-7 (juvenile) primary feathers of *one* wing can be clipped to prevent the birds flying out until the adult feathers grow.

learn that the pen is a secure base before flying out to face the rigours and dangers of the free world outside. There are some shoots, particularly in the far north and in Scotland, where better recovery rates have been achieved by releasing full-winged poults at eight to nine weeks of age. In this situation either a large pen can be used and the young pheasants let out very carefully and quietly into a thicket so that they do not try to fly on liberation from the crates. Alternatively a pre-release pen may be built with a netting roof to house the birds for a few days. Then the door should be surreptitiously left open one morning so that the inhabitants can trickle in and out at will, but without disturbance. Where very large pens of several acres are used this technique can pay dividends. It can be a help in preventing young poults becoming disorientated and lost or separated from food and water. If intensively reared birds, which have received only a sparse period of 'hardening off' are released, it may be advisable to include a large covered area as a sort of night shelter in part of such a pre-release pen.

It is most important to ensure that all bits have been removed before release. In addition, most gamekeepers also administer a light de-beaking. The stress and strains of being caught, crated and transported from the rearing field to the release pen is often enough to initiate a bout of feather picking or, more commonly at this age, tail pecking. Once in the relative freedom of the release pen it is normally impossible to catch up the poults to deal with any outbreak of trouble and so the common attitude is that a precautionary upper beak clipping is worthwhile. There is a small extra advantage in that if anti-feather picking bits have been used in the rearing stages then the upper mandible grows with a slight curve. After de-beaking it will re-grow to a more normal shape.

Transporting the poults is important. They must be kept well ventilated but not exposed to draught. Extremes of temperature can be disastrous and therefore a prolonged period in something like the back of a car in direct sun must be avoided. Most game farmers have their own specialist wooden slatted boxes for carrying birds, and the poultry industry has produced some excellent and very hygienic plastic crates.

Sadly, one of the most vital factors to aid success is beyond control. Obviously young pheasants have a far greater chance of survival if released during a period

Poults are normally transported in well ventilated wood or plastic crates. They should be liberated carefully and quietly into a sunny area where food and water are provided.

90

of warm dry weather. On this score one can do little more than listen to the forecasters and pray. This is one area where the home producer has a distinct advantage over the shoot buying in poults because there will be the option of holding the birds back in the rearing units until a settled spell. Game farmers have a short season and therefore may not be able to offer such an opportuity because they may have another batch to fit through the equipment.

Ex-laying stock

Because pheasants do not lay as well in their second season, gamefarmers and shoots which produce eggs finally offer the adult birds for sale or release them. Sadly, tagging experiments have generally shown poor recovery rates (average of about 15%) from these liberations although there are the occasional exceptions.

Birds which have been caught up and penned for the laying months and are released back onto the same shoot sometimes survive reasonably well. The greatest disasters have been witnessed when stock, which has been held over winter and therefore never experienced the wild, are released onto a shoot where predators, particularly foxes, are not under adequate control. The birds are probably not accustomed to roosting off the ground and if tipped out without the protection of a pen and electric fence are a perfect gift to any large ground predator.

It is significant that many of the reports of good returns from ex-layers have come from areas which are fox and feral cat free. In this situation not only have up to 60% of the birds been harvested during shooting, but in hot dry summers there has been evidence that some of the hens laid small clutches from which they hatched a brood of chicks. If the birds are released before the middle of June, there is a greater chance of some of these youngsters surviving.

Releasing through a pen will give the ex-layers some oportunity to acclimatise gradually to the wild. If the birds have been kept in an open-topped laying pen on the shoot the simplest system may be merely to remove the brails so that the birds can fly out, but continue feeding in and around the pen area. It is important not to wing clip laying stock that is intended for release. The pheasants will not be full-winged again until after their moult in the months July/August.

Birds that have been kept in netted aviaries can be released through an open-topped pen as described for poults, but there may be a disease risk in using the same area for both. Also the adult birds still in and around the pen when poults are released can be aggressive and may bully the youngsters. It is therefore desirable to make a separate pen for the ex-layers, but no primary wing feathers should be cut because of the delay until the moult. Five or six outer primaries on the wing may be pulled to ground the bird, because this will result in replacements starting to grow immediately. Alternatively a pen with a top should be used.

Where there is no woodland, closed topped pens are sometimes used for releasing poults. The control of ground predators must be accordingly strict because of the lack of roosting.

Releasing through roofed pens

In addition to releasing full-winged adults after laying, closed-topped pens are sometimes used for releasing poults. In areas where there are no trees, such as parts of the Fens, it is futile trying to educate young pheasants to roost. They will 'jug' at night and the control of ground predators must be accordingly strict.

Pens made either of sections well bedded in at ground level or some rolls of wire mesh erected together with a roof net can be handy for releases directly into cover crops or reedbeds. The birds should be fed for a period of a few days until they appear settled. Then a number of birds are let out every few days. This leaking process continues until all the birds have been liberated.

Feeding must be maintained in the area but eventually the sections can be moved. Even with an electric fence round the pen the risk of predation to birds spending the night on the ground outside this protection is enormous, but in some parts of Continental Europe where birds of prey can be a problem, especially when passage populations pass through at release time, a pen with a top is essential.

Marking birds

Decisions on the future management of a shoot where there is annual restocking are most likely to be correct if made with accurate knowledge of past results. In the first few seasons this means that marking birds prior to release is essential. It

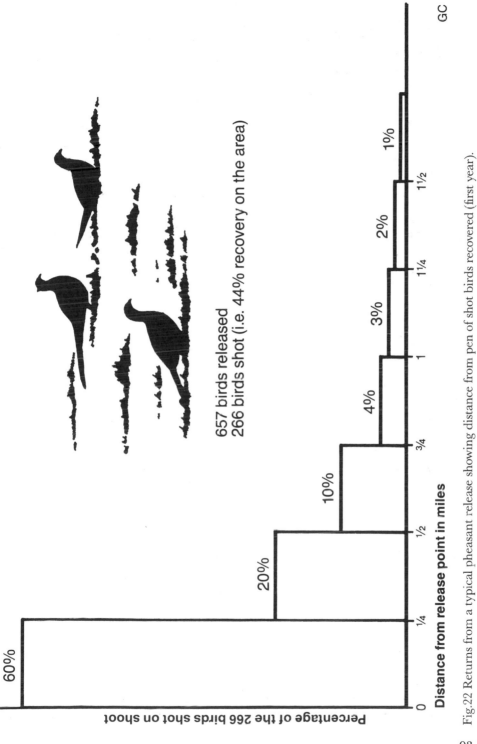

657 birds released
266 birds shot (i.e. 44% recovery on the area)

Percentage of the 266 birds shot on shoot

Distance from release point in miles

Fig.22 Returns from a typical pheasant release showing distance from pen of shot birds recovered (first year).

GC

is astonishing how often observation is proved completely erroneous when tested by a tagging or ringing campaign.

For generations 'keepers and shooting people alike were of the confirmed opinion that cock pheasants tended to stray more than hens. Certainly the colourful cock is much more easily seen wandering over the boundary than the relatively dull feathered female, and perhaps this is what led to the generally false assumption. From study after study, it has now been found that it is normally the hen that has the greater tendency to migrate. This fact alone can have great management implications on future restocking policy, particularly when linked to the previously mentioned possibility that reared hens do not make as good mothers as the truly wild birds. Obviously releasing cocks only, which is likely to result in less straying, will also leave a breeding stock composed only of wild hens together with immigrants.

On the individual shoot more basic information can be gleaned from marking birds. If more than one release pen is chosen then the recovery rates from each will indicate where there is greatest scope for management improvements. One shoot, which had been releasing for several years, recently took Game Conservancy advice and tagged their poults. The results revealed that although the annual bag was 60% of the number of birds released, three-quarters of these were wild birds and immigrants and that the actual recovery rate of reared birds in the first season was no more than a miserable 20%. This was bad news perhaps, but at least steps have now been taken to remedy the situation instead of carrying on an unsuccessful restocking programme in blissful ignorance. The deliberate head-in-sand ostrich-like attitude of not tagging because of not wanting to know the terrible truth is extremely common although frequently camouflaged, with a host of dubious excuses such as 'the time it takes to put them on', cost, and even lost applicators!

The actual physical operation does take a few seconds per bird. Catching the poults for de-bitting, wing clipping and de-beaking will normally be necessary and therefore extra time or added stress should be insignificant. Tags now cost in the region of £5 per 100 which is very good value when considered against the advantages of the increased and certain knowledge gained. Rings are not generally recommended for pheasants because they can become trapped over the spur of the cock bird, causing an abscess or growth. For partridges or duck this problem should not arise, and one advantage of a ring over a tag is that it can be seen when the bird is close or being observed through field glasses.

Occasionally reports are received of tags falling out. This can happen but invariably the cause is inept application in the first place. Special pliers are required and it should be remembered that Ketchum applicators are not suitable for Quadtags. The pliers are made to close to a certain distance ensuring that the tag has a secure fit without damaging the bird. It is important to remember to leave some room for growth on the wing of the young bird. Do not therefore place the

The wingtag should penetrate only the loose flap of skin in front of the 'elbow' joint, and room should be left at the leading edge of the wing for growth.

tag tight up to the leading edge of the wing. It is vital that the tag penetrates only the loose flap of skin in front of the 'elbow' joint and avoids any muscle or bone.

There is certainly little purpose in marking birds if records of their recovery are not kept with care. To ease such taking of statistics it pays to tag different pens with one of the six different tag colours available and, if possible, to alter colours each year. For more detailed identification tags can be supplied printed with a letter code and in consecutive numbers. At the Game Conservancy, where the objectives are to conduct scientific research which can be translated into sound practical advice, careful collecton and monitoring of tag returns is vital. The same can prove invaluable on a shoot.

Taking tags off after individual drives is the simplest system. They should then be placed in a suitable tin labelled with the beat number and drive name, so that the information can be tabulated and processed in peace and quiet at a later date. There is normally plenty to think about during the actual shoot without having to worry about clip-boards and long lists of numbers.

Management after release

It may take anything from a few days to a month for wing clipped poults to 'go over the top' of a conventional open-topped pen. It depends on how hard the birds were clipped, the size of the pen, the height of the wire and the age at release. It is vital to use the period of confinement to the pen to maximum advantage. Not only are the young pheasants acclimatising to the wild, but they should also be familiarising themselves with the pen as a safe 'home' area and in particular with the feeding system involved, which should be the same as that to be used later in the coverts.

Once the birds can fly out there are only three real weapons in the 'keeper's armoury to hold them: good habitat; feeding; and dogging in. If the former is unsuitable then the entire job is going to be difficult if not impossible. Cold, exposed coverts will not hold pheasants for long, once harvest is over. Even worse, if young poults evacuate the pen in any numbers before the corn is cut there can be tremendous losses either directly to foxes and ground predators or through birds becoming disorientated and lost in the sea of standing crop. Cereal stubble on the other hand is ideal in the vicinity of a release pen because it provides a wonderful foraging area for the poults, but at the same time they can see around and also be seen if they are wandering too far. Sadly, with modern agricultural trends towards more winter corn, pheasants and partridges alike must make the most of an all too brief period of stubbles. If not actually incinerated they seldom last long before the plough, chisel plough, or cultivator are turning them over ready for the following season's crop.

It is at dawn or after the morning feed that pheasant poults normally make their first exploratory sortie from the pen. They are often drawn east by the morning sun (as the old 'keeper's saying goes). Certainly in large woods they are likely to be attracted to a sunny area which, unless there are suitable rides or clearings, means they will migrate to the edges. In the early stages they will normally make the return journey in the evening, for food, of course, but also with the intention of roosting in the safety of their pen. Poults may find their own way through the re-entry funnels and anti-fox grids. If time allows it is valuable to give them help with a little careful shepherding for the initial week or two.

During the critical 2-3 weeks acclimatisation period while the wing-clipped pheasant poults are restricted to the pen they should become familiar with the feeding system and the pen as a safe home base.

As with the sun, natural foods also play an important role in leading young poults in a particular direction. Oak acorns and beech mast are unlikely to be falling until later in the year, but fruits like the blackberry in the south and the blueberry on high ground can entice pheasants as well as the public. The tell-tale signs of purple tinted droppings is testament to the popularity of these hedgerow and moorland titbits. Although at this stage of the season insects are no longer so essential for wild game survival they too can entice pheasants far and wide. In particular during afternoons and evenings big hatches of crane flies are frequently wafted over the field by brisk breezes in late September/early October. These are often pursued by large parties of wild pheasants as well as reared poults not long out of the release pen. Ditches and streams are often busy with insect life in a dry autumn and can be guilty of luring birds along their banks and off the shoot.

Such natural influences are often difficult to overcome. With reared birds the main hope for the part-time 'keeper may be to concentrate on drawing the poults back to the release pen and roosting area each evening. Careful hand-feeding, trying to ensure that the pheasants are always a little hungry is the key to dragging birds back. However, if stubbles, hedges and streams are laden with natural provender many people lose their nerve and are tempted into over-feeding.

An alternative approach is to continue feeding the birds with a high proportion of pellets and delay the gradual switch over to grain. Although even covert pellets, a relatively low protein ration specially designed for feeding birds after release, are significantly more expensive than wheat, the extra cost may be worthwhile. Birds will often return to the feed ride for a protein pellet when they might not have done so for a meal of cereal which may also be available on a neighbouring stubble. The other advantage of feeding pellets late into the season is that they are nutritionally superior to grain and therefore birds should make faster and better growth.

For those who can make more time available to 'keeper their shoot in the vital autumn period the other main way to deter the straying pheasant is to use a dog for some careful driving home. Dogging-in on some shoots is absolutely critical to holding game. It can also prove an excellent way to 'tune up' hunting dogs prior to the main shooting season. Pheasants tend to use similar leak or escape lines every season and often at the same time each day. If they are seen meandering along a belt, hedge, ditch or stream, which is thought to be dangerously close to the boundary, an attempt at chasing them back can be made. If possible the birds should be kept on foot and therefore the dog kept back while the undergrowth is gently tapped out. If the dog is too keen the young pheasants may be forced to take wing and they may fly in an undesirable direction, especially if they have been previously dogged a number of times.

9 Flight Ponds and Inland Duck

Everyone has his personal preference and opinion of good shooting. For many, a dusk duck flight has more appeal and excitement than any day at driven game, possibly because of its inherent unpredictability. In most cases mallard and teal are likely to be the main targets of such sporting sorties, although of the diving ducks, tufted and pochard are featuring increasingly in inland wildfowl bags. With the gravel industry producing many new areas of deep water these species are becoming more common. Other quarry species, generally less numerous inland, but which may be encountered especially near the coast include widgeon, pintail, shoveller, gadwall, and goldeneye.

Feeding for an evening duck flight

The mallard is a greedy creature, and the key to attracting it is through the belly. If there is a reasonable population of duck in the area and a suitable sheltered and secluded water area then the duck's habit of flying out for a feed as darkness draws in can be used to devastating effect. It is the duty of all who have such ponds, lakes, streams or parts of rivers to show moderation because it is often possible to lure large numbers of duck to a flight with the possibility of overshooting. In some areas there are a large number of ponds fed for evening flighting and in these it is important that different owners are aware of a reasonable ration that each might shoot. This will vary annually.

The ideal feed is probably barley, and poor quality or tail corn is excellent because a greater proportion of it is likely to float on the water surface. Food should be distributed into the bays and shallow margins. Mallard can only reach 23 cm (9 in.) down when up-ending, while teal can only dabble to 13 cm (5 in.) at the most. Regular feeding is vital - every single day – as close to the estimated time of arrival of duck as possible. The part-timer who dumps heaps of corn in and around the water's edge every few days will normally experience terrible wastage to moorhens, coots, small birds and maybe even rats. However, there are alternatives to grain which are more suitable for intermittent feeding. Potatoes are much favoured by both geese and duck, although they prefer them in a state of decay or when they have become soft after frosting. One 'keeper's trick to make good spuds more palatable for waterfowl is to part-boil them until they are slightly mushy. A few years ago during a dock strike, one of the Game Conservancy

Poor quality or tail barley distributed into the shallow margins of the pond shortly before dusk is excellent for attracting duck for an evening flight.

consultants suggested to a client that he should take advantage of some rotting bananas available for anyone prepared to collect them from the quayside. The mallard poured into this particularly smelly delicacy, although the pond retained the aroma for a full year afterwards!

For those who have corn cleanings, but not the opportunity to feed them each evening, the Parsons Automatic Feeder is a splendid help. It can be rigged up to feed an hour or so before dark, throwing the food into a shallow bay. A collar is available which deflects the grain in one direction and the clock only requires re-winding once per fortnight. The caller bell or hooter can be disconnected, and it may pay to drape a hessian sack over the hopper because the bright coloured galvanised metal has been known to frighten wild duck.

The time of year to start feeding does vary according to location and, in particular, longitude. Young duck fledge at about eight weeks and once harvest is near they may begin to make flights to the ripening corn. Therefore, in the south, it may be necessary to start feeding in early July, while further north, mid-August may be appropriate.

In addition to taking care not to over-exploit the local or even a migrating population it normally pays to rest an evening flight pool for at least three weeks between shoots. This should allow time for the duck to build up confidence to return to the pond on a regular basis. Rather than rely on a time gap one can count the numbers flying in each evening to obtain a better idea of when it will be safe to arrange a flight. However, success will also depend heavily on the weather conditions for the evening. A rough, windy night with limited moon and good cloud cover are the customary ingredients for exciting sport.

Stubbling ducks

Just before and for a period after harvest it is sometimes possible to have some interesting evenings duck shooting, either on the ripening corn or on the consequent stubbles. In areas where there are high mallard populations significant agricultural damage can be done to cereals both by duck feeding and also by their trampling as they waddle through the crop.

Once the precise spot where the duck are feeding has been identified by reconnaissance it is a matter of laying an ambush at the appropriate time. This is normally an hour or two before dark, but in the late summer mallard may flight to such places much earlier in the afternoon. An alternative to shooting the actual landing spot is to shoot the flight line. This should disturb the birds less and therefore may work for a greater number of outings. Observation is vital to locate the exact line in different winds and, in particular, which positions the duck pass over within gunshot. Again, a windy, stormy night is ideal to keep birds down, and also to dampen the shot sounds which on a still evening can dissuade any following parties.

Habitat features for a duckpond

A pond or water area for duck does not have to be particularly big. A pool dug to Game Conservancy advice some years ago which was no more than 30 m (33 yds) across would regularly draw in over 500 mallard on an evening flight. Large expanses, in excess of 100 m (110 yds) across are often difficult to shoot because the duck learn to circle the area out of range before dropping down like parachutists directly into the middle. Even where driving is intended the birds can gain height well out over the water area before passing out of range over the guns hiding a short distance back from the banks.

The depth of a pond can be critical. In fertile parts some deep areas of 1.2 m (4 ft) or more are required to insure open water which passing duck can see and land on with ease. There is a tendency for shallows to colonise with reeds and rushes, some of which are highly invasive. Reedmace, which is what most people think is a bulrush, is a very bad culprit in this respect. Around the margins shallow bays are ideal, both to provide shelter with the vegetation that grows in them and also as feeding areas. If big numbers of duck are likely to dabble in these shallows it is worth tipping some rubble or gravel in to make a hard base which cannot be

Large expanses of water are not so suitable for flighting. Where duck tend to drop down like parachutists directly into the middle, building hides in the water may be the answer.

Fig.23 The ideal evening flight pond has a shallow island with gently sloping banks, surrounded by deeper open water with shallow sheltered bays at the edges for feeding.

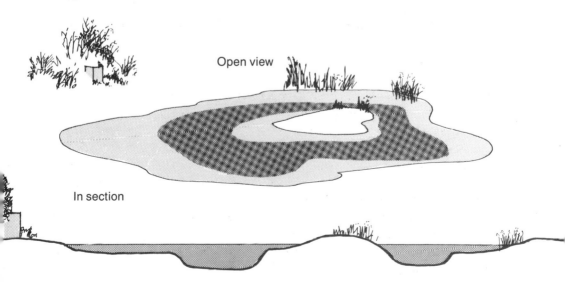

Open view

In section

101

(Left) If big numbers of duck are likely to dabble it is worth making a hard base in the shallows to prevent erosion.

(Right) Stock must obviously be fenced out of any planted areas!

eroded. A shallow island with gently sloping banks up which duck can wadde without effort will make useful loafing places relatively safe from ground predators.This assumes they are far enough from the main banks to dissuade all except the most enthusiastic swimmers such as the mink.

While shelter from wind and disturbance are important, too many trees around or overhanging the water can make it difficult for duck to fly in and out. Shrub species are often of more use than trees in this respect, but even they should be planted several metres back from the water's edge. The occasional groups planted on the margins and trained to grow into clumps overhanging the water can make useful cover, but too many may one day give problems for picking-up. Stock must obviously be fenced out of any planted areas. Powerlines close to a pond have been known to put duck totally off an area previously favoured by them.

A stream flowing through will be useful in hard weather in reducing the chances of the pond icing over. In these conditions such places can suddenly become very popular with many different species. Indeed, streams and rivers can quickly yield dividends, especially if a quiet bay can be fed.

Releasing mallard

In an attempt to 'put something back' into the wild duck population which they are harvesting many shoots consider releasing mallard. They are certainly easy to rear but there are risks involved in liberating any quantity of birds on an evening flight pond. A few, perhaps a dozen, as decoys should not pose a problem. However, large numbers of reared duck can bully their wild cousins. They are also likely to hoover up all the food so carefully scattered each evening before the flight of local birds arrive.

Releasing duck on a pond that is not shot and then feeding them to another

102

Fig.24 Ponds in woods can be particularly suitable for duck drives. Guns can stalk into position unnoticed while tall trees help to ensure sporting birds.

area which is flighted can work well. If predators are adequately under control mallard can be let loose directly. Normally, however, they are penned at or near the water's edge at about eight weeks of age so that they have a week or so to acclimatise to the area before fledging. Their considerable greed makes it easy to hold them around a pond after release, but to gradually convert them into 'wild' duck can take considerable skill.

Controlled feeding and exercising are required in a delicate balance. Too much food and the mallard will soon become so fat that they are almost incapable of take-off. Too little and they may choose to fly elsewhere. Feeding them gradually away from the release pond, especially up a hill or through tall trees, and then chasing the birds back is one technique that can be useful in making them use their wings.

Ponds in woods are particularly suitable as duck drives or even for producing mixed drives with pheasants. The guns can be placed with tall trees between them and the pond, which means the birds have to clear the trees before they are in shot.

Recovery rates from stocked duck are often very high (up to 90% of marked birds released), but unless great care is taken the quality of the shooting can be much less successful.

10 Releasing and Driving Partridges

Reasons for releasing

Over the past fifteen years the Game Conservancy have conducted considerable research into the decline of the English partridge. Some have even criticised the amount of resources devoted to this work, but the old 'keepers' saying that 'if you look after the partridges, the rest will look after themselves' contains much truth. Sadly, it is now appreciated that with a much changed and more efficient agriculture, a loss of game habitat, and a decline in the number of professonal 'keepers, many areas can no longer support a big enough partridge population for organised shooting. Where there is suitable cover, the pheasant has taken over as the main quarry species. In many parts, in order to produce the traditional early autumn shooting, it is now necessary to supplement the partridge population by restocking with English, French or a mixture.

The native bird is preferred by most for its flying ability, its excellent and determined parenthood, its call in the countryside, and even its culinary flavour. However, the Frenchman has its assets, being rather more easily reared and handled in captivity and having a tendency to cross the gun-line in small groups. It also seems at home with the modern autumn arable farm conditions of plough, cultivated ground and winter corn. For walking up, the redleg can provide rather poor sport, preferring to remain a pedestrian instead of bursting up in front of hunting and pointing dogs like the grey. The choice of species or indeed whether to try a mixture will depend on the habitat, the contours, the farming system, and what sort of shooting is required. For those embarking on a new venture it will pay to call in an experienced consultant rather than learn the expensive way - by trial and error!

Release pens

There are a number of different types and sizes of pens which have been successfully used for partridge releasing and a simple and suitable unit can be made from ordinary game rearing equipment. Four 3 m (10 ft) sections tied together at the corners and covered with a soft roof net will accommodate twenty-five poults with comfort. For a smaller number a similar unit can be made to ground measurements of 3 m (10 ft) by 1.5 m (5 ft) from rearing sections. Redlegs

The redleg seems to be more at home with the modern autumn arable conditions of plough and cultivated ground than the grey partridge, which prefers the stubble and root crop.

are great diggers and so pens set out for them should be carefully bedded into the ground. In addition, a shelter, a suitable hopper, and a drinker, should be provided both inside and outside the pen. Partridges do not generally respond to hand feeding like pheasants, and the Game Conservancy recommend a hopper leant against a bale so that the feed slits are at an angle and about 25 cm (10 in.) off the ground. The birds constantly jump on to the straw bale and call, which helps the partridges inside the pen to communicate with those outside. This is helped if the hoppers are sited adjacent to each other. Another way to encourage the liaison is to turn one or more sections upside down so that the wire netting runs nearly to ground level. This also gives the birds a view of their surroundings in addition to any of their fellows who have already been liberated. Care should be taken not to reverse a section on a particularly exposed side because the shelter normally afforded by the bottom boards is then lost.

Partridge poults, both English and French, have been successfully acclimatised to the wild at a variety of different ages, but from recent studies it would appear that birds of 9-11 weeks old survive best. Certainly it pays to wait until harvest is over because reared poults can quickly become lost in standing corn. Also ground predators can stalk up on them with ease. If straw is to be disposed of with the 'Ronson baler' then this should be completed before putting birds on the shoot. Stubble fires will often scare partridges and drive them off the ground. In fact, disturbance of any sort should, where possible, be minimised.

(Left) Four 10 ft sections tied together at the corners and covered with soft roof netting will accommodate at least 25 poults.

(Right) A shelter, a suitable hopper and a drinker should be provided both inside and outside the pen.

Siting the pens

The siting of partridge release pens can prove critical to the success of the restocking operation. Apart from boundaries there are other geographical features which play an important role. For driven shooting maximum use should be made of any contours and so releasing each side of any valleys may be the ideal. Where it is possible to produce double drives this should be attempted because it is often easier to split 'coveys' into small parties on the return when it is driven back immediately, before the birds have had time to re-group.

Tall hedges are useful not only for showing partridges but also for providing a sheltered area in which to site the release pen. Similar shelter may be afforded by game cover crops such as maize, sugar beet, or kale, and certainly where game strips meet plough, stubble, winter corn or even grass there is often a suitable situation for a pen. Pit holes which abound in some areas make excellent release sites, and the rough ground under pylons has been most successfully used on one Kentish farm where Game Conservancy advice was taken with the result that an indifferent pheasant shoot turned into one of the most successful driven partridge shoots in the county with a mixture of both grey and redlegs.

Disruption to acclimatising partridges caused by essential agricultural activities has already been mentioned. In addition, disturbance from natural predators, cats and dogs, or just people, will quickly scare reared partridges off a shoot. It is therefore important that predators are adequately controlled and it is vital to select release sites as far as possible from public rights of way. Where stock are likely to be allowed into a field during the releasing period it is essential to fence the pens. Otherwise cattle and sheep will rub against them, liberating the birds prematurely if they don't actually break the sections.

One of the key differences between French and English partridge is that the former can be flushed in small groups by skilled driving much more easily. It is therefore possible to release them in relatively large groups or in pens that have been sited close together. Englishmen have a greater tendency to pack and are much more difficult to show over a line of guns a few at a time. It is normally advisable therefore to try to release coveys of English well apart from one another and if possible so that the birds in each pen are out of sight and sound of their neighbours.

Releasing procedure

The releasing procedure is remarkably simple. It is no more than a gradual leaking process of birds from the pen, normally over a period of a few weeks. If a 'covey' of 25 birds is placed in a pen then five or so may be liberated within two days. They should be anchored to the pen area by their fellows still in captivity. If they are seen to remain in the area and seem contented then a few more can be allowed out until after about ten days just five or so 'caller birds' remain in the pen. It is normal practice to hold these birds for about a further week until the released birds appear firmly settled in the area. Then the callers can be released and the pen removed but at least one hopper, one drinker and a shelter should remain. If the partridges have been reared under hens or bantams then the fowl itself can be used as an anchor instead of the caller birds.

If conditions are correct the birds leaked out should be held in the pen area by their coveymates still in captivity.

Where there are a number of pairs of grey partridges which have failed to produce a wild brood it is possible to release poults close to them. Often the barren pair will move in quickly to adopt them, and such foster parents usually prove successful in introducing the reared birds to the wild.

If there is a shortage of releasing equipment it is possible to refill the pen and liberate another batch through the same unit. However, care must be taken when actually letting out partridges a few at a time. There is nothing worse than seizing a fistful of birds and dropping them out of the pen door. They are likely to fly a considerable distance and they may never return. A pophole in one corner of the pen attached to a length of string leading to the opposite corner is a help. The pophole should face into some ground cover or special crop. In this way exactly the required number of birds can be allowed to amble quietly out of the pen with no shock or fright.

Once the final birds have been released a further period of a few weeks should elapse before the first shooting day. The birds will continue to acclimatise to the wild at the same time as they become familiar with their new surroundings. This should ensure that they fly well and provide testing shots on the very first shoot day, be they redleg or grey partridges.

Partridge driving

Although the partridge season opens on September 1st driving rarely begins until mid-way through that month and often in arable areas where harvest is late it is October before a start is made. Sadly, there are few shoots today where wild partridges are sufficiently numerous to make organised driving worthwhile, without bolstering stocks with some reared birds. There can be no doubt that good controlled presentation of driven partridges is an art. On occasions it may be possible to produce an excellent pheasant drive with a mixture of the guns' wives, children, and friends wandering through a covert, tapping their sticks. The same team would require some years to develop the timing, technique, skill, and experience required to direct coveys of grey or redleg partridges from a stubble or root crop over a tall hedge so that there is a good distribution of testing birds over the whole line of guns.

For many gamekeepers, shoot owners and managers alike the satisfaction of laying on a good partridge drive in a stiff breeze is amongst the most rewarding of experiences. For the newcomer there are a number of basic principles to consider but perhaps the most important are the birds' natural flight lines, the weather and in particular the wind, the cropping and hedge pattern, and, of course, the topography of the ground.

There is little future in attempting to drive partridges on a line in which they persistently refuse to go. While experience of the ground is necessary to discover the favoured ways in which the birds will fly it is astonishing how accurate a picture

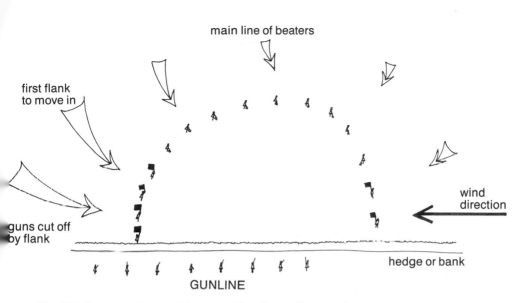

main line of beaters

first flank
to move in

guns cut off
by flank

wind
direction

hedge or bank

GUNLINE

Fig.25 Measures taken to drive partridges in a stiff cross wind.

can be built up by walking the ground alone and flushing a covey or two in different weather conditions and observing the line that they take. This may not be the same direction from one year to another.

The second factor, cropping, may well be a major influence. The position of stubbles, if there are any that have not been incinerated or ploughed, and root crops in relation to each other, is particularly significant. To split coveys or packs of greys into small groups a field of roots, turnips or sugar beet can be invaluable, while redlegs by contrast can frequently, with careful flagging be flushed in ones and twos even from bare plough.

Sadly, not every shoot is blessed with undulating ground, but where there are slopes it is vital to make the most of them. In particular reared redlegs really require some gills, banks or valleys to show at their best. On flat land and in heavy clay country on a wet or very hot still day they can earn a poor reputation as testing quarry. However, the same bird in a strong wind on steep downland can catch out the most demon deadly shots. The grey is normally capable of giving a good account of itself even on level ground providing there are some tall hedges to position the guns behind so that the coveys burst and flare on the opening shot as they top the obstacle. In addition to using low ground to fly birds across it should be remembered that both partridge species, like grouse, are often contour fliers. They tend to prefer to drift downhill on hanging wings in the classic manner. Therefore if drives can go with the slope of the ground so much the better. This will also help in that the beating line or circle should be in view of the birds, making their direction of flight easier to control by flagging.

The final factor is normally the least predictable of all. Even the Weather Centre

On steep ground with a good breeze released redlegs can prove testing, even for the best of shots.

The grey partridge is normally capable of giving testing shooting even on level ground if there are some tall hedges.

Butts should be constructed several weeks before shooting so that birds have time to be accustomed to them.

can be wrong and minor deviations, particularly in the direction of the wind, can be absolutely critical. Partridges will fly downwind and can often be driven straight into a moderately strong breeze. It is a cross wind that can most seriously affect driving and it is important to preserve the option to move a flank or alternatively move the gun-line. It can, on occasions, be necessary to have the line of flankers move right across some guns and cut them off! When this happens it is obviously vital that the guns know, not so much because they may think they are being deliberately starved of sport, but mainly because of the more important safety precautions.

On a first day of driving on a new partridge shoot, preparation will be vital to success. A walk of the drives with the captain of the guns, the head of each flank line, and one or two key beaters to talk through the operation a few days before will pay handsome dividends. An extra point which can help is to explain to all the beaters and flankers that flags are more likely to turn partridges if shown suddenly. Therefore they should not be carried dangling over the shoulder or waved continuously as though royalty was expected at any minute.

Butts, which may be necessary in open country to conceal the guns, should be constructed several weeks before the shoot so that birds have plenty of time to become accustomed to them. Hurdles, hessian stretched between fence posts, a heap of bales, will all make simple, natural looking hides.

Finally, a good loud thunderer-type whistle carried by both flankers can be a great asset. On many drives there is a long wait before the first birds burst over the gun line and a sharp shrill blast can work marvels at waking those guns who are dozing off or becoming engrossed in the antics of the neighbour's unruly dog or other companion.

Fig.26 Partridges flying out of a drive turn best if flags are waved suddenly. Flankers should therefore be alert and watching the approaching beaters, not the shooting.

11 Winter Management and Feeding

The need to feed game

Many modern farms and woods can prove to be hungry habitats for game and wildlife in winter. Today there are generally fewer hedgerows and untidy corners with their autumn larder of insects, berries, and weed seeds than in the past. As already mentioned, the shift from spring corn to increased acreages of winter cereals has resulted in most of the stubbles being either incinerated or ploughed-in directly after harvest in readiness for autumn drilling. Many of the copses, spinneys, and forests planted over recent decades have been composed mainly of conifers rather than the seed- and fruit-bearing hardwoods.

By management of the wild stock through effective predator control, the provision of good nesting cover, and sympathetic farming which should help to produce good chick survival, the autumn population of game on the shoot may be artificially high. The same situation may have been caused by releasing birds. In either case it is most important that extra food be provided to supplement that which is naturally available if these birds are to remain on the shoot and a stock survive through the winter in good condition for the following spring.

There are two equally important aspects to the making of such provisions. First, there should be an even distribution of suitable habitat which offers both food and shelter. The use of special game crops can be an important method of compensating for a shortage of permanent cover and may also provide food in certain cases. Second, and often much easier to arrange, is the direct provision of food for game by hand, hopper, or automatic feeder.

The pheasant feed ride

Whatever system of feeding is adopted on the shoot, the areas chosen to feed should provide a number of essential comforts. Of course, attempts will be made to draw birds up to high ground where they can be shown well on shooting days, but if the feed ride is sited in a cold draughty place it is unlikely to prove successful.

Pheasants love the sun and plenty of light will help to keep the area dry. Therefore a ride running north to south will generally be preferred to one running east to west, especially in tall woodland. In some areas a very open feed ride can be troubled by birds of prey. All are, of course, protected by law but that does not

February and March are often the hardest and hungriest months for gamebirds. Feeding should continue, both to hold breeding stock and to maintain their condition prior to egg laying.

mean that some species do not occasionally take a gamebird. More serious is the fear which their presence near or over an open feeding area may cause. The disturbance can prevent pheasants from venturing out on rides, in which case an area in dense cover may have to be adopted instead.

Ground predators, although less obvious, can also disrupt feed rides. Plenty of escape cover nearby will make pheasants feel more secure, therefore a margin of low shrubs along each edge is ideal. The Game Conservancy recommend plants which hold their leaves for most of the winter such as creeping privet, *Lonicera*, laurel and even bramble, because all give good cover. Often too much attention is devoted to planting berried shrubs. In reality, a dozen pheasants could devour all the berries off a host of plants in a matter of days. It is simpler to provide the food itself out of a hopper or bucket. The second reason for requiring good shrub cover at the edges of feeding areas is for shelter from weather and, in particular, the wind. Again this is best achieved by evergreen species. As a short-term measure cover and shelter can be provided by laying branches and tops of trees in lines alongside the ride, but this will involve a considerable amount of work and the effect seldom lasts longer than one season.

No feed ride should extend to the very edge of wood or crop. This will only allow the wind an opportunity to blow through, and possibly prying eyes a view

(Left) The pheasant feed ride. Sun, shelter and escape cover are all important when siting a pheasant feed ride.

(Right) Feed staddles, shelters alongside the feed ride, with light soil underneath make popular dusting and scratching places.

of what is on the ride. In creating a new feeding area it is best to cut a winding path rather than a straight line. Again this should reduce wind and draughts, but also later in the season when cock pheasants become increasingly territorial one may dominate part of the ride, chasing others away. With a number of twists such an aggressive bird will not be able to see all his competition.

On a driven shoot the direction of the drive may affect the line the feed ride should take. Some 'keepers like it to run across the drive, but this can encourage big flushes. A feed area cut to wind through undergrowth along the length of a drive with cover on its margins is more likely to produce a good spread of birds throughout.

In a dry area water can be very important. This is particularly relevant where reared birds are involved. They have been accustomed to being fed on dry protein pellets and having water supplied. If water is not available they may wander miles in search of it and this may mean off the shoot.

Feed staddles will definitely be used if they are supplied. They should be constructed along the edges of the rides in sunny areas where there is some light dry soil in which birds can dust. On heavy soils some heaps of wood ash under the shelters can encourage pheasants to take a dust bath, which is known to help in removing feather vermin such as fleas and lice. A simple staddle can be made from a matt of straw sandwiched between two layers of wire netting. A good size is 3 m (10 ft) square and about 0.6 m (2 ft 6 in.) off the ground. Alternatively, a double-decker can be made with a corrugated iron roof protecting the strawed centre section. In this case the straw may be loose. The birds will enjoy scratching it off each day in search of the odd grain.

To make the ideal feeding place for pheasants one should consider the needs and likes of the birds and aim to pander to them. After all, holding game is about limiting their enemies, making the habitat suitable, providing adequate food and water, and every extra little comfort is likely to make your shoot a better place than next door.

115

Hand feeding pheasants

There is little doubt in the minds of most professional gamekeepers that hand feeding is the best way of holding pheasants on a shoot. However, the daily commitment involved on a large acreage to carrying out the job correctly for the six or seven months over which game commonly requires supplementary feeding is considerable.

The big difference between the hand and hopper operation is that the latter involves making food available to the birds while the former is more about rationing it. The objective therefore should be to keep the pheasants hungry or sharp so that they feel that need to return to the 'keeper for breakfast, supper or whatever the next feed-time is. Quantity control is one of the keys to success.

The pheasant is very much a creature of habit. It will rapidly become familiar with a routine. Once used to feeding at a certain place each day it will report for grub with monotonous regularity. If the 'keeper misses a day or two it will not be long before the pheasants lose faith and begin to wander. It is also important that once a regular pattern of hand feeding has been established that the feed is given at the same time each day. A pheasant appears to have a time clock in his belly, governed more by hours after daybreak and before nightfall than the watch.

Hand feeding, spreading the grain or pellets and calling must be regular and punctual to be effective.

116

If labour is available for two feeds per day then this makes it easier to draw birds to certain areas or coverts at certain times which can be fitted in with shooting day plans. As a general rule any cover crops and traditional morning woods should be fed after dawn while release pens (if they are still being fed) and evening areas are more eligible for an afternoon feed. In this way, the birds should be drawn to the outer coverts and morning drives during the day. They should then return to be fed in the warmer and hopefully safer roosting areas before dusk.

Because pheasants become familiar with a system they can be called to the feed. The secret of success is an early training in the feeding tune. Most 'keepers whistle their birds up, and start accustoming the poults to their particular tooth noises in the rearing field. Of course, not everyone has teeth and a surprising number of people cannot whistle. This really matters very little because any sound which carries for a reasonable range will suffice. Some bang dustbins, others purchase gongs, horns or thunderer whistles. If pheasants are hungry and know the meaning of the chosen sound, they will come scurrying to the feed. Fortunately, after a few weeks birds can also recognise the 'keeper or person feeding them so there should not be any great danger of a poacher imitating the noise to his advantage.

Reared birds will probably be fed mainly on protein pellets at release, but on most shoots they will be gradually weaned off these and onto grain, (initially kibbled or soaked), which is much cheaper, particularly if the farm has put aside a few tons at harvest. Pheasants have rather expensive tastes, much preferring wheat and maize to barley, while oats is a very poor fourth. By the autumn a considerable sum of money will have been invested in the shoot and it does not pay to try to skimp and save by cutting corners at this stage. Pheasants should be fed the best grain. Tail corn can be kept for the ducks or for when the shooting season is over and holding a stock on the ground is the main intention. The one case where barley is adequate is when no wheat is grown in the area and no-one nearby is offering the birds wheat or maize. There are certain other foods which pheasants greatly relish. Currants or sultanas, tic beans, even peanuts, are popular but they are all generally too expensive to be cost effective as the standard ration. Often maize is not fed because of expense, but on occasions it can be purchased for less than wheat. Whole maize can also become the most economic ration where sparrows and small birds are frequent visitors to the pheasant feed ride because they have difficulty in taking the large niblets.

Feed storage and straw

The quantity of food that even a relatively small number of gamebirds can consume over a season is quite considerable. From the Game Conservancy's Game Shooting Cost Analysis figures the average grain consumption for 500 pheasants from release until the following March when feeding is likely to cease

Storage bins (and stacks of straw) strategically sited can greatly reduce the burden of carting by hand to each feed point.

is 4 tonnes. This amount obviously varies according to the season, natural food, acreage of food strips such as maize, the weather, and also shooting policy.

However, it is still a hefty weight to cart about the shoot. For the amateur and professional 'keeper alike it will probably make the task easier if storage bins can be deposited at each feed place and a cross-country vehicle used to deliver the grain to these every two weeks or so. Sometimes old deep freezers can be purchased for very little and if hidden away in woods can be excellent for storing pheasant food. Often they have locks, which can be necessary in areas where the local back garden poultry flocks are owned by the light-fingered. Alternatively an old 200 litre (45 gallon) drum with a specially made top can make a weather-proof container. It is certainly a lot less effort to dip a bucket in at each feed ride for grain than to have the arduous task of walking around the shoot under the burden of a ½ cwt sack.

In wet woodland areas storage bins may be more of a necessity than a luxury in that the autumn rains render the rides impassable to all motorised transport. In this case it will be important to ensure that sufficient straw has been stacked on the feed rides to last the winter. The value of straw in helping to hold birds is often grossly underestimated. Firstly, pheasants associate it with stubbles and feed so it proves a natural draw. Where cattle are fed hay it is amazing how quickly gamebirds will be in evidence, scratching about for food like farmyard fowl even when there is no grain involved. With reared pheasants it will pay to make a thin fresh layer of straw along the feed ride in the release pen so they become thoroughly familiar with it and its association with food.

The second value of straw is the fact that many small birds such as sparrows, starlings, and finches, traditional robbers of the pheasant feed area, are not able to scratch and therefore will be denied their normal quantity of the expensive corn. Even pigeons have a limited ability to find food concealed in a bed of straw.

Linked to this is another advantage. It takes the pheasant longer to fill the belly when each grain has to be hunted for in litter, and the longer the bird is kept searching on the feed ride, the less time it has available for wandering away and possibly over the boundary. Of course, there are other things which can be used as litter, and some 'keepers consider a good bed of dry leaves a suitable alternative although they are not as eye-catching as a fresh, fluffy strawed ride to the passing bird.

There is one danger posed by the use of straw. Particularly if old or damp it can be liable to contamination by a fungal disease called *Aspergillosis*. Very occasionally birds which have contracted this ailment are sent in to the Game Conservancy pathologist. However, it is relatively rare. If fresh straw is used and reasonable precautions are taken there should be no real danger. Straw should be kept stacked on the feed ride and be protected from the weather by a securely tethered polythene sheet. Only thin layers should be spread along the ride, but frequent fresh applications will make it more attractive. If at the end of the season the remains are damp and have not rotted down, then it is a simple matter to rake them into heaps and, providing there is no fire risk, burn them up with the help of a little diesel.

Hopper feeding

Many part-time and amateur 'keepers have difficulty finding the time each day to hand feed their coverts on the regular basis so essential for success. Full time 'keepers are often in charge of so much ground that a number of outlying areas cannot be serviced daily. The commitment of hand feeding may be possible to honour during the summer, but when in the winter the day-light hours become fewer the programme may have to be cut and hoppers substituted in some places for the job to remain practical.

If the birds are to be fed by hopper at any stage then it is vital that they have an opportuity to learn how to use them. This can be achieved with reared birds by installing a few in the release pen at a suitable height so that the poults can feed from them. If rearing from day-old chicks it is even better to introduce hoppers to the rearing units for a week or so before release. Where regular hand feeding is to be the main system to be used in the coverts then only a few hoppers should be set up in the release pen for the familiarising of young poults. Otherwise there is a danger of the birds topping up from the hoppers and not responding adequately to the call.

Training wild stock to hoppers is a little more difficult in the first instance. The main hope is through the use of skilfully sited feed areas and plenty of fresh straw to attract the birds. By placing the hoppers in sunny, sheltered secluded spots where game tends to congregate and scattering some grain in the straw under each one, it should not be long before even the most cautious of old campaigning cock pheasant catches on. Once one generation has hoisted in the message then the following season's wild youngsters soon pick it up from their parents during the increasingly hungry months after harvest.

There are some pheasant shoots where the birds are deliberately fed by hopper in preference to hand feeding even when time for the latter is available. The theory

Hoppers require careful siting, particularly for wild pheasant. This position has the shelter of a yew tree, and plenty of fresh straw has been spread to attract the birds.

behind this practice is that birds not accustomed to being fed by a person each day should remain in a more wild state. The next step in the argument is that these birds will fly better when flushed by humans or driven over them. Like so many theories it is difficult to conclusively prove or disprove, but certainly on flat land every possible aid to better presentation may be worth pursuing. However, a certain confidence that pheasants are not likely to stray is usually required because the invaluable knowledge of the birds' well-being and where they are on the shoot that is gleaned from their regular reporting to the hand feed is sacrificed.

Partridges of both species rarely respond to a 'whistle up' call and hand feed. Consequently a network of strategically sited hoppers is often considered the most effective feeding system. Redlegs, in particular, will join pheasants on feed rides, but they frequently lurk back in the bushes until the 'keeper has gone before venturing out with confidence. The grey is generally even more shy and for birds with this type of behaviour it is difficult to see any advantage to hand feeding over the simpler and time-saving hopper techniques.

Once a feeding system is adopted it pays to decide on one that can be continued right through the season. Changes from hand to hopper or wheat to barley should be avoided. If a particular type of feeder has been chosen it should be used as the standard for the whole shoot. Where pheasants are released, hand feeding of the central and more accessible areas may be possible with hoppers installed elsewhere. When considering the lay-out of the hoppers on a feed ride it is important to remember that a number of birds may wish to feed at the same time and, as already mentioned, as the season draws on so pheasants become increasingly territorial. Therefore it is totally inadequate to have one or two hoppers in a wood where it is hoped to hold a hundred or more birds. As a rule of thumb guide at least one hopper should be provided for every ten to fifteen birds expected to feed at a place, be they pheasants or partridges. This may require a few more hoppers than was originally envisaged. The time that their manufacture takes should be more than saved later because the hoppers will require topping up less often.

Making hoppers

There is a great range of different types and sizes of gravity hopper on the market. Many have been given field tests by the Game Conservancy Advisory Staff and most have proved quite adequate. However, with the purse strings of most shoots under considerable tension, it seems more sensible to devote a few hours to making hoppers. This is very simple and typical farm utensils such as the ubiquitous 25 litre (5 gallon) drum or bigger vessels are excellent. If possible, metal containers should be chosen as wood and plastics can prove popular to rats, mice, and squirrels, all of which will quickly gnaw through them.

The first operation will probably be to clean the container, for many agrochemicals are highly toxic. If water-soluble, a thorough soaking and rinsing operation should eventually do the trick. When dry it pays to give a lick of rust preventative paint to both the inside and outside as this can double the life span of the hopper. Obviously to paint the inside the top must be cut off and this can be done with a sharp metal chisel, a jig-saw, tin snips, or with gas cutting equipment. Some prefer to leave the top on and fill the hopper via a funnel through the small tophole, but if blockages occur these are then difficult to clear. If the top has been removed a new lid must be made from a sheet of metal wider than the diameter of the drum. By bending over the excess metal a clip-on top can be made. A heavy rock on top of this should ensure that even a gale will not blow it off. Alternatively the ends of similar sized plastic drums can be cut to slide over the open end as a tight weatherproof top, although even these can be vulnerable to the above mentioned rodents. The nearest thing to a perfect lid can be made from the individual discs of a disc harrow. The centre hole should be plugged with a piece of wood which will double as a handle. The convex shape of these discs allows water to run off while their weight is sufficient to hold them firmly in position. Sadly, a derelict set of such harrows is not always to hand. Perhaps the perfect container is the old milk churn, and with bulk tank transport now the common system for moving milk from farm to dairy one can occasionally pick up old churns. These are particularly suitable as game feeding hoppers, being both rustproofed and waterproofed.

The business end of a hopper is normally sited in the base. When grain outlet channels are cut in the side, problems inevitably arise in wet weather when rain is driven in by strong winds. Once damp, the corn will germinate and within days lumps of solid, intertwined seedlings will probably have clogged the apparatus. Therefore, it pays to make the feed area in the actual bottom unless the hopper is to be sited underneath a shelter.

Some 'keepers like to use some sort of mesh, such as very small gauge weldmesh or several layers of wire netting sandwiched together. These are adequate but liable to robbing from small birds, many of which can hang on to the grid while feeding merrily on the hopper contents. Squirrels, rats, and mice also find mesh easy to hold. The Game Conservancy therefore normally recommend one or more simple

(Left) A mesh base hopper allows birds to see the grain, but small birds and squirrels find it easy to hang on while robbing the contents.

(Right) The Game Conservancy anti-sparrow guard has a slit protected each side by flanges. A pheasant or partridge beak can reach the food but small birds cannot hover underneath.

slits just wide enough for the grain to pass through. Provided the hopper is always reasonably full, the pressure of grain on such a slit will prevent it from actually running out. During some observational trials at Fordingbridge on the causes of losses from gravity hoppers to non-game species, sparrows and squirrels were found to be the most serious pests. The former learnt to hover under the slit while thieving from it, and squirrels hung onto the slit with one 'hand' while clawing grain out with the other.

As a result, the anti-sparrow guard was invented and manufactured in conjunction with Quadtag Ltd. This is a metal plate with suitable sized slit through which to feed pellets or good wheat but which has protective flanges mounted on each side. These allow a pheasant or partridge to peck grain while making it difficult, if not impossible, for small birds to hover underneath. Sadly, squirrels were not to be defeated. When the hopper is post- or tree-mounted they have difficulty in reaching the guarded slit. Instead they were observed climbing onto the hopper and then performing a bouncing act which caused the odd grain to fall to the ground. They would then descend and enjoy consuming this before repeating the process. However, as already described in Chapter 4, grey squirrels can be controlled by trapping and poisoning.

One system by which even rodents can be outwitted is to suspend the hopper by some wires. This is relatively easy if the feed ride has some suitable overhanging branches. Of the other mammalian robbers (apart from farm stock which obviously must be fenced out from the feed area), deer are the most likely source of trouble; although not nearly so serious as wild boar which can be a great

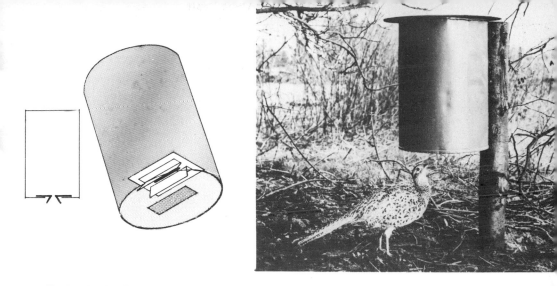

(Left) Fig.27 The Game Conservancy anti-sparrow guard is designed to slip into a hole (6 x 2 in.) cut in the base of a suitable drum.

(Right) For adult pheasants the feed slits of a hopper can be up to 43 cm (17 in.) from the ground.

problem in parts of Continental Europe. The importance of taking some precautions in deer country was emphasised recently on a shoot near Fordingbridge when a roebuck was seen crossing a woodland ride with a 25 litre (5 gallon) pheasant hopper perched like a top hat on its antlers. One simple solution which usually dissuades roe is to mount the hopper on the side of a scrub tree and to staple about five strands of barbed wire above it, each one radiating down to a peg firmly driven in the ground.

The mounting height of hoppers is very important and for adult pheasants the base or feeding slit can be up to 43 cm (17 in.) from the ground. This will reduce the chances of pigeons and corvids reaching them. Of course, when introducing hoppers to reared pheasants in a release pen it is necessary to reduce the height to about 30 cm (1 ft) so that poults can use them with ease.

Partridge hoppers

Hoppers suspended from branches or mounted on posts at the correct height for pheasants are unsuitable for partridges. They cannot reach to 43 cm (17 in.) off the ground and from observation it appears that they prefer to peck at a slit or mesh that is nearer to the vertical than the horizontal plane.

A satisfactory solution to these differences is to use a similar drum with feed slits cut in the base, but to mount it so that it hangs from a stake or post at an angle of about 45° to the ground. This can be achieved by leaning it against a straw bale. Redlegs, in particular, enjoy jumping on the bale to survey their surroundings and give their characteristic 'chuk-ar, chuk-ar' call. This is valuable at partridge releasing to aid communication between birds inside and outside the pen. The

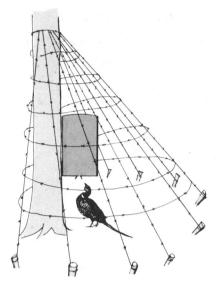

Fig.28 Strands of barbed wire forming a cone round a hopper mounted on a tree should deny access to hungry deer, but will allow gamebirds to feed.

actual feeding slits should be between 20 cm (8 in.) and 30 cm (1 ft) from the ground.

There is some danger of moisture entering the drum from rain driven by strong winds. The risk of this can be reduced by ensuring that the slits face away from the prevailing weather, or by siting the hopper in the lee of a protective hedge. Alternatively, the entire area may be covered with a shelter. In fact, the provision of a dusting shelter near partridge feed points can prove very popular with the birds. A sheet or two of corrugated iron securely propped up on a bank which will catch the sun is all that is required.

One advantage of home-cut chiselled slits is that they can easily be reduced or increased in width by a few taps of a hammer from one side or the other. This can be of special value when feeding partridges, birds which often take time to become adept at pecking for the food. Making rather large slits initially can help them discover the technique, but once they have got the message it pays to reduce the size otherwise the over-enthusiastic birds can adopt hopper emptying as a game, which is both tiresome and expensive. The other advantage of variability in slit width is that cracked wheat, seconds, or even tailings can be fed through the hoppers if required later in the season, while the much larger pellets can be given to released poults earlier in the year.

A drum hopper suspended against a bale at an angle of 45° with the feed slit or mesh 20-30 cm (8-12 in.) off the ground is suitable for partridges.

124

A simple 25 litre (5 gallon) drinking fountain can be made from farm waste.

Drinkers

As already mentioned, wild pheasants will manage to find water naturally from ponds, puddles, and even dew in the early mornings. Reared birds, however, which have been accustomed to having water provided, must be able to drink freely particularly if they are being fed on a proportion of game or poultry pellets. A shortage of drinking water for released poults may well lead to straying, or even worse it can cause death. If water is made readily available at feed points both wild pheasants and partridges will take advantage of it.

One common danger, where sheep and cattle water troughs are sited near release areas, is for young poults to perch on the edges to drink from them. Unfortunately all too frequently the foolish young birds lose their balance, fall in and drown. If there is any risk of this the troughs should be temporarily covered with netting. If livestock are in the fields concerned then two or three large rocks onto which the poults can scramble should be placed in each trough. In fact agricultural water troughs can be handy sources for the shoot. It is a simple matter to connect an alkathene pipe to such a supply for automatic drinkers. Alternatively, they may offer the closest available water with which to refill home-made fountains.

A simple and successful drinking fountain can be made from farm waste. A circular 25 litre (5 gallon) plastic or metal drum is required with the hole slightly recessed from the top, together with a rectangular plastic jerry-can container. Both

125

should, of course, be rinsed and thoroughly cleansed. The latter should then be cut longitudinally to produce two shallow trays of 9 cm (4 in.) deep. When the round can is filled with water and inverted into one of the shallow trays a convenient long-lasting water dispenser is made at little or no cost. The water will flow from the drum until it covers the opening, then it will cease until more water is drunk or evaporates. An added advantage of such devices is that further water can be carried easily by vehicle in the same drums when replenishment is required.

Another technique to provide water is to dig a shallow trough in the ground and sink a polythene sheet into it before refilling with earth. This is important because sunlight and frost can quickly destroy the plastic. Such depressions will collect a little water during wet spells, as will a motor car or tractor tyre split in half. An old-fashioned method of ensuring they receive extra rainwater is to tie a length of plastic binder twine around a nearby smooth-barked tree and to attach a rock to the other end. The rock is then placed in the drinking place so that the string is under tension. Water running down the trunk will tend to collect on the string wrapped around the tree and then be led down it to the pool. A depression of any size should have one or two big rocks in it, to prevent the chance of young birds drowning. The problem with these systems is that, unless the pool is deep, the content is likely to evaporate during a prolonged dry spell, when a water supply is most vital for gamebirds.

Automatic feeders

The shorter daylight hours of winter can pose problems, particularly for the part-time 'keeper. Those with a regular nine-to-five job who also have the responsibility for feeding birds may suddenly face an impossible task to tend to their shoot duties when summertime ends. There are a number of mechanical automatic devices which can perform a close approximation to a hand feeding routine. Although they may seem relatively expensive to purchase, the man hours saved over a season is often ample reward for the financial investment.

The best known and longest standing machine on the market is probably the Parsons automatic feeder. This is available in two models, one with a 500 kilos (half ton) fibre glass hopper, the other of 120 kilos (2¼ cwt) capacity is made of galvanised metal. The former is possibly more suited to the feeding of hill stock on inaccessible ground, with the latter more commonly used on shoots.

Some of the basic aspects of hand feeding are incorporated in its performance. The control box allows for a selected quantity to be fed at the turn of a knob with a variation from about 1 kilo (2 lbs) to 13 kilos (28 lbs). If more is required then a double feed is simple to arrange. However, the area over which the revolving spinner distributes the food is limited to about a 10 m (33 ft) diameter circle. In Game Conservancy field tests some years ago it was found that this was suitable

The Parsons Automatic Feeder (2¼ cwt) model on trial at the Game Conservancy. Time and quantity of feed can be controlled and there is a caller.

KIRKLEY HALL

for no more than 150 pheasant poults in a release pen. Greater numbers of birds tended to become over-concentrated with some unwanted aggression resulting. The main expense of the unit is the control box but a number of hoppers and their distributors can be linked with wires to operate off one box.

Timing of the feed is another important feature. The robust 24-hour clock requires hand winding once a fortnight. A small screw is placed into this opposite the selected feed time or times. This screw depresses an electrical contact at that time to activate the feeder. Recently an electrical time clock has been developed as an alternative to the clockwork one. This is slightly cheaper and means that the fortnightly winding up is not required.

Power to drive the distributor is supplied by a 12-volt heavy duty car battery which, if fully charged, should last up to three months depending on the number of feeds per day.

The final similarity to hand feeding is the caller system. This can be a bell or hooter, the latter being of a pitch designed and tuned more to the pheasants' hearing frequency than that of humans'. In trials, birds were seen coming to the hooter call from up to half a mile on a still day. The call will operate for a good length of time regardless of the feed quantity and delivery period.

Grain or pellets can be fed through the Parsons, and a special screen is available to fit to the hopper so that tailings with the odd bit of straw can be fed without clogging the distributor. Automatic feeders are particularly suitable for out of the way evening flight ponds where, as described previously, 'duck suppers' should be provided ideally every evening an hour or so before dark. Two important modifications may be required for wildfowl. A covering of hessian or a coat of dull paint may be necessary as the bright galvanised metal has been known to scare them, while the directional baffle may be helpful to make the machine feed into the shallows.

A number of other automatic feeders are now on the market. The R.G.S. and the East Anglian Shooting Products exhibit a number of similarities. Both have a light sensor to trigger the first feed of the day which is given soon after daybreak, subsequent feeds being given at an adjustable interval throughout the day, with the option to give just the one at dawn. Both also allow variation of the feed amount, and have a buzzer to call the birds. Since the dawn feed cannot be prevented, these feeders are not really suitable for duck flight ponds.

The East Anglian has the facility to adjust the diameter of spread of food between approximately 10 m (11 yds) and 15 m (16 yds) and could probably supply rather more birds than the Parsons. It also has a strong but lightweight fibreglass hopper, while that of the R.G.S. is in heavy plastic, and might be susceptible to damage by rats or squirrels.

Whichever machine might be chosen by a shoot it is important to remember that, being valuable and reasonably portable the feeders and their battery are obviously liable to theft or vandalism. Also reared birds accustomed to such devices can become so familiar with them that they disregard hopper or hand feeds in neighbouring coverts.

12 Organising the Shoot Days

Long-term plans

If the main intention is to produce walking up or rough shooting for one or two guns who are close friends and in regular contact with one another, then preparations can be left very much to the last minute. Where more formal presentation is the objective then some forward planning is essential. In a sense, plans for shooting days begin to be laid when the sites for special cover crops are being considered, which is sometimes eighteen months earlier on a modern arable farm. Certainly, where restocking is involved, figures must be known so that sufficient birds can be penned for egg production unless day-old chicks or poults are being purchased. Gradually all the individual aspects of shoot management lead from one to the next until by mid-summer it is time to be giving thought to the arrangements for the final product, the shooting days. Once the grouse has heralded the start of another game season plans should be in progress for the lowground. Actual dates should have been decided so that any guest guns can be given plenty of opportunity to accept their invitations. On professionally 'keepered shoots there may be a number of days which are being sold to outside parties to recover some of the costs. The best of these are often booked several seasons ahead.

The size and scale of each shoot will depend on the nature of the ground and on the main target species for that day. Almost before a young wild partridge can fly and before any reared birds are released for the season it will have been necessary to make a number of preparations for their driving or walking up. Special crops and the sparing of certain stubbles from the plough must be planned with the farm months ahead. If a full complement of fifteen or twenty beaters and flankers or pointing and setting dogs are required then it will pay to book them early. This particularly applies in areas where there is a good partridge population. Traditionally, farmers comprised a heavy proportion of the shooting fraternity and mid-week shoots were common, with many tractor drivers and stockmen enjoying a day's beating. Now that the sport of game shooting is practised by all denominations, classes and types, Saturday has become the prime day in many areas with the result that competition for beaters can be severe. It is normally possible to find enough people who will enjoy a day's beating but, with partridges, a surfeit of undisciplined children is unlikely to result in a controlled flow of coveys over the gun line!

Flankers, in particular, must be skilled in the careful use of the flag to turn birds

For driven shooting the number of beaters required for a day will be determined by the biggest drive.

and know the ground. After a season or two, most shoots will build up a team of regulars but in the first year at least half-a-dozen knowledgeable enthusiasts are necessary to manage the drives if the remainder are novice beaters.

The number of beaters required for a particular day will be determined by the biggest drive. On a formal pheasant shoot the stops are often as important as the beaters, and in well-hedged or heavily wooded ground more stops than beaters may be required. Because they spend much of the time out of sight, there is a terrible temptation to detail the most stupid and least experienced beater for stop duty. This is a profound mistake, for a stop is likely to have to remain alone at the position and may have to take important and instant decisions. Therefore, while no great athlete is necessary, a level-headed person and not the village idiot should be selected.

Experienced pickers-up with good dogs are often in great demand, and so to obtain the best it pays to make arrangements months in advance. It is astonishing how many shoots fail to employ enough pickers-up, which in these times of increasing scrutiny of field sports, must rank as a most important aspect. In fact, it is quite amazing how many times an efficient team of dog and handler will pay for themselves by extra birds found.

For pheasants there may be some physical preparations required to ensure that the coverts are ready for shooting. Brambles, briars and undergrowth will all have grown up during the summer, and some tracks may need opening up with a slasher or even a tractor and swipe. This work is better tackled in the summer or early autumn rather than waiting till nearer the shooting day because the birds themselves will find woods more accessible if some paths have been cleared. Too many beaters' paths can be a mistake in that the less enthusiastic follow them rigidly rather than thoroughly tapping out the bushes. At the same time, stiles should be installed for both guns and beaters where they are going to have to cross fences. Wrapping hose-pipe or sacking around the offending barbed wire may suffice. It is this sort of attention to detail that shows up the top, thoughtful, industrious, amateur or professional 'keeper from the average.

If partridge driving over a stand with little cover for the guns then butts may need to be built (as mentioned in Chapter 10). These should be sited at least three weeks before shooting. A line of hurdles or other similar materials can be as off-putting to partridges as a line of guns if the birds have not had time to become used to them. Bale hides, especially on stubbles, can be erected closer to the shooting day without such danger.

To some, these early preparations for the forthcoming season may seem tedious, but for most it is a sign that after all the hard work the fun is about to begin. If things have gone according to plan then making the long term arrangements should be the start of an exciting if nervous build-up to the final product – a successful and smooth run shooting day.

Final preparations

For the professional and amateur 'keeper alike shooting days are the real judgement time when during a mere ten or a dozen days over a period of three or four months the results of the entire year's labours will be revealed.

The 'keeper's life was once described as 350 days of worry working for those dozen or so shoot days when terror and blind panic take over. It is therefore important to do everything possible to ensure that the final preparations are perfect.

The guns, beaters, pickers-up, should all have been invited and booked months ago, but a quick telephone call to check should set the mind at rest. For those who are expected to bring a dog it is particularly valuable as bitches come on heat and all working dogs can suffer injuries. In the early stages of the shooting season the cover is at its thickest and flushing birds may depend on the spaniels and terriers much more than the human beaters.

In real thicket country, as already mentioned, tracks will have been cut to give access for the birds as well as the beaters. Flushing tracks may also need to be opened up where sewelling is required so that birds rise before the end of a drive. Before the first shoot the forked sticks on which it is suspended should be cut and positioned at intervals along the track. The traditional system for flushing pheasants was to use rabbit netting, but this can have two disadvantages. Birds which are constantly trying to bash their way through netting can injure themselves, and running along the wire and beating against it exhausts the pheasants. They have a limited amount of energy and it is important to try to channel all of this into strong flight so that they provide really testing shooting.

Sewelling consists of a length of strong string or cord with 5 cm (2 in.) wide and 1 m (1 yd) long strips of coloured plastic attached. Fertiliser bags cut longitudinally are ideal and should be joined to the cord about every 24 cm (9 in.) by a clove hitch knot. It is a simple matter to make up 90 m (100 yds) on a quiet evening, the actual length required being determined by the widest drive on which it is going to be used. The sewelling should be hung across the drive at the position where it is intended that birds should flush. The forked sticks on which it is suspended are placed on a cleared track at about 3 m (12 ft) intervals and at such a height that the strips actually brush the ground. It is rare for even a reared pheasant to run past sewelling correctly made and set up if a person is at one end of the line giving the string a gentle tug to keep it moving. Just occasionally a wily old cock pheasant will jump or make a short flight over it and land the other side rather than leave the covert.

Sewelling lines are normally set out with one or more slight bulges in them so as to lead the birds to these pockets where suitable flight channels through undergrowth and trees exist and where they will spread satisfactorily over the gun line. A further and more advanced use is to angle it across a drive so that birds, when they first see it, are encouraged to run along its length and onto higher

Fig.29 Sewelling should be suspended on forked sticks along a flushing ride. Constantly pulling the string to ensure movement makes it more effective.

Lengths of sewelling wound on to a hose reel are easy to roll up, lay out, and carry from drive to drive.

ground before flushing. Sewelling can also be used with partial success instead of stops for separating adjacent drives. It can be extremely useful in this context along woodland tracks or rides to prevent birds scampering from one block to another.

The effect of sewelling is blunted if it is left up in a wood for a number of days before or after a shoot because birds become too used to it. The sticks on which it is hung may be left out, but ideally the string and plastic strips should only be rolled out just before the drive or, if easier, on the morning of the shoot day. Many shoots where it is used on several drives have a long length which is kept wound onto a hose reel or stick and entrusted to one beater whose job it is to carry it from drive to drive, erect, dismantle and work it. If, despite the dangers, wire netting is used instead then it too must be lifted after drives otherwise it will provide an obstacle to normal game movement and a trap against which birds can be caught by predators.

The positioning of the guns is often critical to the height of the birds. The object, of course, should be to place the guns in a situation where game will have fanned out to give a spread and reached a good height. Direction is also important and it is vital when gunstands are marked out for the first time that both the captain of the guns and the 'keeper or leader of the beaters do so together. It may be that final adjustments and changes have to be made because of wind and weather on the day but this is only feasible if both ends of the operation are aware of the precise positions.

Actual marking of stands is sometimes avoided by the individual placing of guns. This can be risky from two angles. There is always the chance that someone will misunderstand a verbal briefing, but more important, trying to ensure a shot for a gun who has had no shooting all day will invariably result in all the birds flying elsewhere to the increasing embarrassment of the host or captain. Marking stands and drawing for numbers is certainly simpler. By adding two or three to the number each drive (depending on whether there is an odd or even number) the guns should move through most positions during the day. It is quite staggering how few people seem capable of simple addition during a shooting day. In particular, accountants, bank officials, statisticians, and others whose special skills

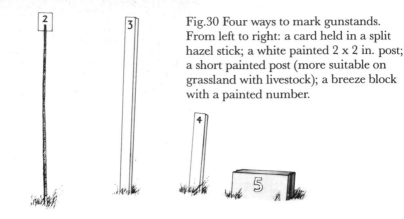

Fig.30 Four ways to mark gunstands. From left to right: a card held in a split hazel stick; a white painted 2 x 2 in. post; a short painted post (more suitable on grassland with livestock); a breeze block with a painted number.

involve numerical activities are often the worst offenders. To help those with amnesia it may pay to give each gun a card with the stand number for each drive written on it. Even this apparently foolproof system can go adrift when someone's card gets dropped in the mud on the way to the first stand. For the bold of heart there are more complicated systems of changing numbers. One involves the even numbered guns adding two or three and odd numbers subtracting two or three. The advantage of this system is that guns receive different neighbours each drive, and it also ensures that no gun is sandwiched between his worst enemies all day!

Card or plastic numbered labels inserted into the split of a stick is probably the commonest system of marking out gunstands. However, stock, in particular cattle, will soon knock them down but metal electric fence stakes which can be pushed firmly into most ground will normally survive cows rubbing. Another sensible system, in this situation, is to paint the numbers on breeze blocks and to stand these up in the grass.

Farm stock, horses, even newly drilled crops may need to be given a wide berth on shooting days. The route and ground covered on each shoot must be discussed with others involved in land management, in particular, farmers, farm managers and foresters. It will also pay to inform any locals who might be affected by the shooting. Most people will appreciate and respond to such courtesy.

Finally some last minute preparations may be required to ensure the comfort of guns, beaters and pickers-up. Transport may be by foot, car, jeep or trailer. The

Positioning of standing guns is often critical to the height of the birds. They should be sufficiently far back from the covert to allow birds to see them and rise.

To attract the best beaters it is worth providing them with some comfort. Cover from the rain and seating will be appreciated on any transport and during lunch.

latter, together with the lunch hut or shed, will be more popular if some seating is provided even if it is only a line of bales. Later in the season a good fire and hot soup will probably be appreciated. It is often the little things that result from attention to detail that put one day's shooting in a class above the rest.

The beaters

Driven shooting is a sport where enjoyment is not restricted to the guns. Many a modern day beater is out more for pleasure and interest's sake than for financial reward. It is precisely this sort of attitude that should be sought in the choice of the team. People who are thinking about what they are doing and why they are doing it are invaluable because shooting is thoroughly unpredictable. A few fit, keen enthusiasts are worth any number of unwilling farmhands who have been press-ganged into service.

Many contemporary beaters also have a gun in a shoot. Such people are perfect because they will understand both ends of the operation. They may also own disciplined flushing dogs, which in thick cover can do the work of a multitude of beaters. Dogs are not always welcome in the beating line. If a considerable number of birds are expected and cover is limited they may be conducive to big flushes. One wild dog can ruin an entire day for everyone quicker than anything. Equally, a few controlled dogs can make a shoot. It is well worth ensuring that any dog that is invited to join the beating line is seen working with game beforehand. No-one should object to such screening.

One system of attracting some of the more enthusiastic type of beater and picker-up is to organise a special shoot for them. It is a valuable way of saying 'thank you' for the essential contribution they make to the success of the season. It also gives them a glimpse of the other side of the coin, perhaps making them aware of the ease with which guns can miss!

The regular beater on a driven shoot soon learns the salient features of the operation and after a few outings on one farm may even adopt a particular role

Beaters should be clothed for comfort. A few yards through marrowstem kale is enough to soak anyone without a waterproof.

on individual drives. For the newcomer, whether a friend or relative out for a day in the country, or someone who is expecting some remuneration for his efforts and travelling time, there are some basic instructions which may be of value.

A few years ago a gun's enthusiastic wife appeared in the beating line on a shoot close to Fordingbridge in a bright red jump suit. Apart from distracting the concentration of a number of the 'regulars' the effect on the coveys of grey partridges was devasting. Thankfully in this country it is not generally necessary to wear day-glo or fluorescent attire to avoid becoming featured in the bag. The important matter is to be clothed for comfort, which will usually involve something not only thorn and brambleproof but also waterproof. Even if it is not actually raining on a shooting day, a few yards through wet marrowstem kale is all that is required to soak those without leggings and wellingtons.

Equipment as such is normally provided by the shoot. Flags, if required, and sticks should be supplied by the 'keeper. Many beaters prefer to use their own, in which case the main priorities are to ensure that a stick is stout enough to survive plenty of bramble bashing and tree tapping. A highly prized carved walking stick is not ideal and may, if used conscientiously, not last many days. Tapping is an important matter. Sometimes the intention will be to make pheasants run from one area to another, probably through the covert to a flushing point. This is known as blanking and can be easily effected by a constant rattling of sticks on trees or even boots provided that there is no talking or shouting. Blanking apart, it is a good principle not to talk loudly during drives unless passing a message along the beating line. Game can hear and shouting normally makes game run to the closest nearby cover and tuck up so that only a dog will flush it. Perhaps the worst audible sin is to make loud and derogatory remarks about the marksmanship of the guns. Remember that they are there to enjoy themselves. Comments like 'he's missed yet another' or 'I could do better with a stick' do little to help the confidence or pleasure of a gun going through a bad spell.

In addition to ensuring all messages are passed along the line, it is vital to listen carefully to and understand all instructions. If in doubt one should always ask rather than continue in the hope that the brief will become clear. Most foul-ups

The golden rule for all beaters is to keep in line.

on a shooting day can be attributed to a lack of communications. On a similar note, if a beater finds a dead or pricked bird during a drive he or she should inform the 'keeper. Otherwise pickers-up may waste hours searching for a bird already safely in the game cart. Obviously it is important to know how to dispatch wounded game humanely and those who are uncertain should ask an experienced person to give a demonstration.

Not every beater will enjoy ploughing through a blackthorn thicket but if it is in their path it must be thoroughly tapped out and prancing around the edge will not be sufficient to ensure birds move on. If the beating line is rather thin for the width of the cover then the team should zig-zag to and fro. When birds flush the line should stop and merely keep the sticks tapping otherwise there is a danger on well-stocked shoots of too many birds passing over the guns at one time.

Perhaps the most golden rule for all beaters be they driving grouse, partridges, pheasant, hares, even woodcock or snipe, is to keep in line. This is doubly important if there are walking guns, whose purpose is often to shoot birds escaping from the sides and going back. In this situation, the 'line' is not just for efficient beating but for safety also.

The bag

After all the work and endeavour of managing and producing game it seems a pity that some pay so little attention to storing it correctly. Particularly on the less formal shoot, pheasants, partridge, even grouse, are often just bundled into the back of a land-rover. Next a heap of wet dogs are thrown in to trample on it followed by those guns not quick enough to make the comfort of the front seats. The result is frequently a sort of game silage of heating corpses with the birds being exposed to plenty of dampness but no air.

The roughshooter's game bag exhibits sections for the two basic requirements for the storage of game on the shoot. Most have a main bag, which will keep the dead quarry dry, and a string netting compartment, which when it is not raining and flies are not a problem will help rapid cooling.

It is important to allow dead game to lose temperature reasonably fast and ventilation is one of the key factors in making this possible. Wetness, however, can make game 'sweat' and this may accelerate the speed at which it deteriorates. It is therefore important to provide something that can be covered by way of a travelling larder. If a vast bag is not envisaged the back of a land-rover fitted with a few bars may be quite adequate. Birds can be braced and strung at the end of each drive and then hung spaced out sufficiently so that plenty of air can circulate freely between them.

By this stage of the season it should not be necessary to provide fly-proof containers although on the grouse moors and partridge shoots earlier in the year special panniers may be essential.

The bigger shoots often have a game cart, a vehicle or trailer specially fitted with hooks or rails and driven by a person whose sole responsibility for the day is to collect the bag from each stand. Several years ago one of the Game Conservancy staff devised a simple carrier for the smaller shoot. This was a modified game cart roof rack designed to hang over the top of a four-wheeled drive type vehicle. It provided for good ventilation and also had canvas flaps as rainproof covers, and of course the inside of the vehicle is left free for dogs and people.

If time allows it is best to examine the bag while bracing and hanging it in the field. Badly shot birds should be separated so that they are not given to guests or sent to the game dealer. Furthermore, for grouse and partridge, ageing the bag is important as young birds command a significantly higher price than old. Even if no sale is intended it is important for the host or 'keeper to have young birds readily available to give away to guns in a hurry to leave at the end of the day.

A roof rack type game cart allows the bag to cool quickly and canvas flaps can be lowered to keep rain off. Inside, the vehicle is free for dogs and people.

Wingtags should be removed at the end of each drive and dropped into labelled tins for analysis later.

Ageing is a simple exercise which takes only a matter of seconds for most species. Basically, young grouse and grey partridge can be identified by their pointed two outer primary wing feathers. These are rounded on old birds. Redleg young usually have a creamy white tip to the outer primary which vanishes after the first season. Pheasants are a little more difficult. Most people consider that the length of the spur is sufficient guideline for cocks but this has often proved erroneous. A more accurate way to age a pheasant, be it cock or hen, is by the bursa test. Young birds have a small blind hole on the dorsal side of the vent. A match stick or feather can often be pushed about 6 mm (¼ in.) up this orifice. Old game birds have no bursa. Of course, at the Game Conservancy, knowledge of such techniques are vital for data gathering and research purposes but it is surprising how useful information collected on the age of the bag and on the reared and wild content can be of value when considering next season's plans and proposals.

Wing tagging and marking released birds have been mentioned earlier, under restocking. Apart from simplifying the ageing of released pheasants in the bag, it is a relatively futile exercise if the tags are not collected or examined during the shooting days. A simple way to do this with minimum loss of time is to pull or cut tags off birds at the end of each drive and drop them into tins previously labelled with the name or number of that drive. The shoot manager or 'keeper can then go through the tins on a later occasion to identify from which pens birds shot in various drives originated. After a few seasons a general picture will emerge of migrations and recoveries, together with wild percentages on which future shoot management can be based. Once a satisfactory pattern has emerged then future tagging may be of limited value.

Finally, if game is to be stored on the shoot a suitable cool vermin- and fly-proof larder should be available. From reports received in recent seasons, a secure lock may be necessary in many areas. Some thieves appear to have discovered it easier to steal birds already killed, braced and hung up for them than to suffer the cold and sometimes unsociable hours of night poaching!

13 Woodlands and Permanent Game Habitat

Planting and improvement grants and help

The largest single subject on which the Game Conservancy are called upon for advice is the planting and management of game habitat. With the pheasant being the primary quarry species in most of Great Britain the creation of suitable woodlands is normally the top priority. Cambridge University's Department of Land Economy recently published statistics showing that of woods less than 10 hectares (25 acres) 82% are retained as game coverts in addition to other reasons. Furthermore, a similar percentage of farmers and landowners questioned gave this as one of the purposes of recent new plantings.

With the ravages of Dutch Elm disease and an increasing agricultural field size and consequent reduction in hedgerows and rough corners demanded by the large machinery employed on modern arable farms, it is recognised by most professional conservationists that game shooting has always and still does play a vital role in the creation and preservation of some of the most beautiful woodlands, hedgerows, moorland and wetland in the countryside. At the same time, these areas also form important refuges for many other forms of wildlife.

These facts are increasingly recognised and part of the result is that a number of grants are now available to encourage management and new plantings for landscape, amenity, and wildlife purposes, as opposed to purely forestry operations, many of which have long been supported by the taxpayer. Probably the most relevant grant available to those considering planting up small areas on their farm or shoot are those offered by the Countryside Commission, which are mostly administered through the County Councils.

These vary a little from county to county and sometimes the maximum rate can vary within the county according to the importance attached to establishing woodlands in the particular area. However, grants of up to 60% can be available on the total cost of the planting. The requirements to qualify vary a little from place to place but areas up to 0.25 hectares (0.6 acres) are preferred. Some counties will now allow larger areas than this although often at a lower overall rate of grant. The ground should be visible from a public road, footpath or bridleway. (After all, it is public money either from ratepayer or taxpayer that is on offer.) Lastly, native or naturalised species should be planted where possible. This is because they are considered to fit into the British landscape better than non-natives and also because they can play host to a greater wealth and diversity of wildlife species – in particular their insects.

Apart from the inclusion of a few evergreen non-native shrubs for shelter purposes and a moderate proportion of conifers to give cover and roosting for game in the early years of a plantation, the type of lay-out, design and species normally suggested in a typical Game Conservancy copse or spinney can be eminently suited to attracting a high level of grant.

Grant officials are generally very helpful about the establishment costs which may be included in the sum on which the percentage is payable. In addition to the plants, labour and site preparation, fencing or individual treeguards, subsoiling if deemed necessary, and even professional advice on choice of species and lay-out are considered eligible. It therefore pays to 'do the job properly' the first time as financial help is once-off on the initial expense of the planting.

For larger areas where timber production is also a consideration the Forestry Commission Grant Scheme or their Broadleaved Scheme may be more applicable although they are generally less generous. Furthermore the actual payment is made by instalments at five year intervals and operates on a maximum fixed sum. The rate of the former is governed by the overall size of the wood in which the planting is being made and the ratio of conifers to broadleaves planted. The Broadleaved Grant Scheme rate is governed by the size of area to be planted and is particularly relevant for the replanting of existing woodlands where the shrub layer will normally respond to extra light from thinning or felling and produce ground cover for game naturally In this respect the Natural Regeneration section of the grant may also be of particular value for those whose woodlands are managed with game or shooting in mind. Woods with a mixed age structure normally offer the varied habitat requirements of some sunny, some warm cover, and some roosting and shaded areas which are so important in holding pheasants.

Table I showing Summary of Rates of Forestry Commission Grant Scheme (as at Spring 1986)

Area of Wood (in hectares) in which planting	Max grant for conifers per hectare	Max grant for hardwoods per hectare
0.25–0.9	£630	£890
1.0–2.9	£505	£735
3.0–9.9	£420	£630
10 and over	£240	£470

Table II showing Summary of Forestry Commission Broadleaved Woodland Grant Scheme

Area of planting or regeneration (in hectares)	Max grant for: Planting, replanting, or Natural Regeneration per hectare	
0.25–0.9	£1,200	**NB Paid in instalments at**
1.0–2.9	£1,000	**5 year intervals.**
3.0–9.9	£ 800	
10 and over	£ 600	

A five-year plan of operations is required to be approved by the Forestry Commission. Applicants may also be asked to enter into negotiations about public access, but this condition seems to cause some landowners unnecessary disturbance as there is no requirement to enter into any binding agreement.

Another alternative and relatively new source of financial aid for woodland planting is the M.A.F.F. farm environment grant. This offers grants for establishing shelter belts which by definition are an ideal shape for game and other territorial wildlife species of the woodland edge. The percentage grant on offer varies according to the proportion of broadleaved trees included and the geographical area. Basically the grant is doubled for 'less favoured areas', which encompasses the less productive ground, hill farms, and uplands, often where game and shooting play an important part in the rural economy. These M.A.F.F. grants are the only ones available retrospectively, but it is wise to consult your local officials before planting to ensure the site, lay-out, design and species will qualify. Incidentally, the scheme also offers grant aid for the planting of new hedges.

Table Summary of M.A.F.F. Farm Environment Grants re: Shelterbelts and Hedges

Description	Rate of Grant %	
	Basic	Less Favoured Area
Shelterbelts (more than 50% of broadleaved trees)	30	60
Shelterbelts (less than 50% of broadleaved trees)	15	60
Hedges	30	60

For the improvement of existing woodland a number of County Councils are able to offer grant aid for their restoration and management. Operations often of considerable value to game and wildlife habitat such as coppicing (in particular of ash and hazel) and the small-scale clearance of scrub areas for re-planting which frequently makes no commercial sense, may fall into this category. Payment of up to 60% of the cost can be made. In addition, ride clearing, removal of invasive species such as sycamore and rhododendron, and even the opening up of old ponds may qualify for financial or physical help.

In some counties a team of people, often gaining work experience of a new skill but under supervision, is available to carry out hand-work jobs such as clearing old lanes, hedge trimming, or coppicing provided that it is in the 'public interest' (i.e. visible from a public right of way). There are also a number of volunteer groups, of which The Conservation Volunteers is probably the best known, who for a modest maintainance allowance may be prepared to assist on wildlife habitat improvement work.

Planning a game covert

Current Game Conservancy covert plans try to incorporate as many amenity and general wildlife features as possible. This is of considerable importance to the countryside in general because the lengths to which field sportsmen will go to ensure the well-being of their quarry would probably amaze the uninitiated. But it is absolutely critical when diverting farm hectares or even square metres from croppable land to conservation area that the choice of site, design, lay-out, and selection of individual species are all correct. When planting woodlands mistakes may remain to haunt the individual and future generations for over a hundred years!

Siting a new woodland, copse or spinney that is intended as a drive is not always as straightforward as it might seem. Gamebirds don't always obey the rules and behave as expected. Therefore it is a wise precaution to conduct some experiments, using special cover crops, before making the commitment to trees and shrubs. Annual crops such as kale are ideal as a means of checking that birds really will 'cross the valley', 'face the wind', or whatever the intention is. A season's trial with crop will leave the options open to alter shape, width, or length. The only danger is that a wood does not always produce precisely the same results as a crop on a particular piece of ground.

The site may be dictated by the farm in that only ground that is awkward to cultivate, such as damp spots or rough areas, may be available for conversion to new game habitat. Even in this situation a trial crop may reveal that the area does

This two acres of good arable ground was recently planted with trees and shrubs as a permanent game covert. The length to which field sportsmen will go to ensure the well being of their quarry would probably amaze the uninitiated.

Type	Minimum height	Approx. width (diameter)	Suitable for	Effective protection against
a Spiral guard	0.6–0.75m	variable according to tree stem	Hardwood whips and larger	rabbits and hares
b Tree Shelter* (half shelter)	1.2m 0.6m	10cm 10cm	Hardwood transplants Hardwood or conifer transplants	rabbits, hares and roe deer rabbits and hares
c Netguard 2	1.2m	12.5cm	Hardwoods and conifers	rabbits, hares and roe deer
d Netguard 2	0.6m	12.5cm	Hardwoods and conifers	rabbits and hares
e Wire Netting	0.6m	45cm	Shrubs and conifer transplants	rabbits and hares

*Shelters may also considerably improve early growth and survival rates of some hardwoods. Taller models can be ordered for protection against fallow deer, etc.

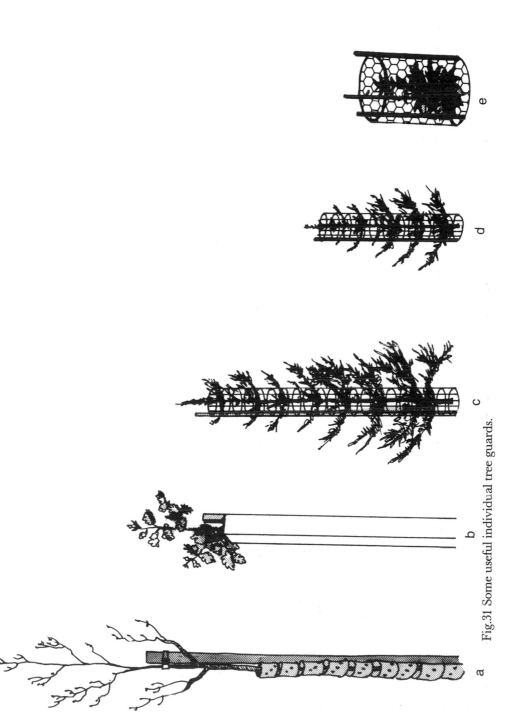

Fig.31 Some useful individual tree guards.

145

By planting tree rows at relatively wide spacing it is possible for a tractor and drill to pass between the rows. Guards make it easy to see the tree lines.

A game crop, such as Canary Grass, grown between the tree rows will be of value to the shoot immediately. The trees and shrubs may take ten years or more to give sufficient cover.

Cock pheasants having a territorial dispute. The number of pheasant territories on an area is partially governed by woodland edge.

not warrant investment into long-term planting for sporting purposes.

Once a successful area has been identified which can be established as woodland then a decision must be taken as to whether plants will require protection from vermin. Rabbits, hares and deer are likely to cause the main problems in the early stages. Wire-netting the entire planting may be necessary. In practice, netting itself is a great deterrent to gamebirds using a new woodland. Pheasants, in particular, prefer to walk rather than fly and therefore access in and out is severely restricted. Individual guards on the other hand are also quite expensive if large quantities of plants are involved, although they do undoubtedly have extra benefits in terms of shelter to the young trees. On balance, it is difficult to justify the use of rabbit netting, let alone deer fencing, as opposed to tree guards around young game coverts which are long and thin or of less than a hectare (2.4 acres), in area.

If individual guards are chosen or if there is no serious threat of rodent damage and wire netting can be avoided, then it may be possible to plant the rows at relatively wide spacing, thus enabling a tractor and drill to pass between. In this situation a cover crop can be grown and maintained to give shooting in the first five to ten years, while the young trees and shrubs are being established. A perennial crop which is not so tall that it will shade out the plants is ideal. Canary grass (*Phalaris tuberosa*) fits this description, while in a reasonable winter, thousand headed kale will survive to re-seed the following year and may last for up to three seasons. Obviously the crop will be in partial competition with the trees, but this disadvantage is often heavily outweighed by the shelter it affords together with the bonus of any fertilizer applied.

Shoot owners often ask how big a covert must be to produce a viable drive. It is similar to that famous question 'how long is a piece of string?'. It depends on the number of birds that are considered necessary for a drive and the nature of the site; the exposure, aspect and surroundings. However, long narrow areas are generally more manageable than square or round woods, and strips are much more practical in terms of the number of dogs and beaters they will require. It is also significant that the pheasant, like many other wildlife species, is a bird of the woodland edge. Game Conservancy research has shown that cock pheasant

Some Useful Herbicides for Forest Weed Control

Trade name	Chemical	Form	Action	Time of application	Main weeds controlled
Clanex (Shell) Kerb (P.B.I.)	Propyzamide	Liquid & Granule	Soil Acting	October to Christmas.	Grass and some broadleaved weeds including buttercups and dock seedlings.
Holtox (Shell)	Cyanazine/Atrazine mix	Liquid	Part Leaf/Soil Acting	England: Jan–April Scotland: Feb–May	Grasses, nettles, willow herb, thistles, many weed seedlings. NOT buttercups or bindweed.
Herbon Lignum	Atrazine/Dalapon	Granule	Soil and Leaf acting	All year, ideally April and May.	Most grasses, including couch, useful effect on nettles and rushes.
Casoron G. (Midox) Prefix (Shell)	Dichlobenil	Granule	Soil Acting	After Christmas in cold weather	Grass and most herbaceous plants. N.B. Douglas Fir, Larch, Poplar, Norway Spruce can be damaged.
Round-Up (Monsanto)	Glyphosate	Liquid	Leaf Acting (Translocated)	During dry weather when weeds are growing	Most weeds and trees except some when completely dormant.
Gramoxone (I.C.I.) Cleansweep (Shell)	Paraquat	Liquid	Leaf Acting (Not Translocated)	Anytime* provided tree is not sprayed (*including hot weather)	Most weeds but generally less complete kill than above. Again trees in leaf are susceptible.

territories are partially governed by the amount of belt, copse, or forest fringe that is available. All indications therefore point to the value of relatively small coverts in belt form being of the greatest value for game.

Looking after young trees and shrubs

It is important when planning a new wood to make provision not just for the planting and guarding but also for management in the early years of establishment. No more planting should be undertaken than can be looked after and weeded each spring. Farmers and shooting folk are frequently enthusiastic at putting in trees and shrubs during the winter months but the agricultural and other pressures of early summer do not always allow the time for the crucial maintainance work.

Hand weeding, with sickle and stick, is the traditional method of freeing young plants from being smothered, but it is time-consuming. If a contractor has been called in to do the planting it may be sensible to arrange for him to continue with the responsibility for weeding for the required number of years to follow. The main months for such operations are from mid-May to late June in the south, which coincides with the peak hatch of gamebirds. It is therefore important that the contractors liaise with the owner or the 'keeper. It may even be worth offering a bonus for any nests found and keeping some bantams on dummies ready to receive hot eggs.

Mechanical weeding may cause more disruption to nesting game if it involves cutting or swiping vegetation between tree rows. In this situation it may be of value to deliberately dissuade birds from nesting in the area and to run dogs through before the actual operation.

Techniques are now available for chemically weeding young trees. A really effective weedkiller which keeps the ground clean through the first half of the summer will produce better survival, height growth, leaf size, and colour than other systems. In addition, some of the herbicides concerned are designed to be applied in the autumn or winter months when more time may be available for the person who has decided to look after a young plantation himself.

The chemicals available in liquid form only can be applied with a knapsack sprayer. Some of these can be supplied with a guard for the nozzle to help keep the spray off the trees. Round-Up and Gramoxone may also be applied with a weed wiper, a simple device consisting of a nylon rope kept damp with a solution of chemical. Many of the liquids may be applied at ultra-low volume (U.L.V.) with a special electric sprayer such as the Herbi and Ulva. These require special expertise, good weather, and careful maintainance. The chemicals which are available as granules may be distributed with a pepper pot shaker (provided by Shell) or with a modified mist blower.

Another useful method of protecting young trees and shrubs from weed

A good farm hedge benefits game and wildlife by providing shelter, food, refuge from predators, as well as nesting cover.

competition is by mulching. This involves spreading a layer of wet straw, bark, roofing felt, or black polythene around the base of each plant. This gives good results because not only are weeds suppressed but also moisture loss to evaporation and weed transpiration are reduced. If the special felt mats are purchased it is an expensive and time-consuming operation. Straw often needs to be replaced each year to continue to be effective, while black polythene requires weighting down at the corners to prevent wind blowing it out of position.

Hedgerows and nesting sanctuaries

The value of hedgerows to game and wildlife can be immense. Good hedges provide direct benefits in terms of nesting cover, shelter from wind and weather, food and refuge, particularly from winged predators. They also form natural travel lines for small ground vermin, which makes control by tunnel trapping considerably easier. The lee of a hedge makes an excellent place to provide winter feed by hand or hopper, and also a sheltered place in which to release partridges. If allowed to grow up to 3 m (10 ft) or more a narrow hedge may be the only place to show driven partridges in a testing manner on flat ground.

A hedge takes many years to grow to maturity, but may be removed in a matter of days. Its beneficial effects may not become apparent until after the damage is

Fig.32 A neat quickthorn hedge on a grassy bank is ideal for game nesting.
A rotavated or sprayed strip may reduce weed encroachment into the adjacent
crop and produces a dusting and drying out strip for birds.

done. There can be advantages to retaining some hedgerows for agriculture as well
as for game. They give shelter to sheep and cattle, which can increase their yield
from liveweight gain or milk production. They act as windbreaks, reducing soil
erosion. This may also help raise soil temperatures and reduce moisture loss
through evaporation.

The type of field hedge most useful to the farmer and the shoot is a neat well-
kept thorn or thorn with mixed native shrub species, planted on a ridge with grassy
banks. Weed control in the adjacent crop is frequently given by farmers as the
reason for hedge removal. However, the provision of a narrow strip of 'no-man's
land' which can be kept 'clean' by cultivation, rotavation, or spraying will reduce
the chance of weeds encroaching into the crop headlands as well as providing
valuable drying out and dusting areas for gamebirds and their chicks. On the other
hand an extension of this useful technique, the spraying of the ground vegetation
in the hedge base, is extremely damaging to game interests and may render the
hedge completely useless for nesting, and as an insect reservoir.

A less obvious contribution of the farm hedge is as an area of undisturbed
ground where beneficial insects can over-winter. A number of the predatory insects
which feed on the agricultural pests such as aphids require this uncultivated
ground, as do many of the species of food value to game chicks. Others live on the
natural mixed weed flora of hedge bottoms.

Recent Game Conservancy research has shown that an average field size of 10
hectares (25 acres) divided by hedgerows is suitable for good wildgame nesting and
is ideal for the grey partridge. In practice the composition of the hedge may be as
important as the overall quantity. A width of between 1 m (3 ft) and 2.5 m (8 ft)
is desirable and the height should not be so great as to risk shading out rough grass
and natural vegetation. Banks of between 1 m (3 ft) and 2 m (6 ft) wide which rise
by between 0.5 m (18 in.) and 1 m (3 ft) to their apex should be sufficient to ensure
good drainage. It should hardly need saying that stock should be fenced out from

Fencing out stock from odd pockets of ground and planting them carefully can go a long way to providing extra nesting cover.

these banks. Plain or barbed wire can be used but sheep netting with small mesh at the base may deny easy access to gamebirds.

Quickthorn planted in a double staggered row with 0.5 m (18 in.) between the plants and 23 cm (9 in.) between the rows and kept regularly trimmed in the early years of establishment so that they bush out at the base are excellent. Other species such as the field maple, wayfarer, guelder rose, and wild dogwoods can be included to add diversity for other wildlife. Hedges which have been laid and are then trimmed by machine will also make good nesting cover.

Once established, an 'n' shape appears to be best for grey partridges and eventually cutting in alternate years is adequate. This should be carried out from July until March if possible. Again Game Conservancy research has shown that too many standard trees in the hedge, more than 12 per kilometre (20 per mile) can reduce their nesting value to grey partridges, although redlegs and pheasants seem less particular.

Isolated areas of cover such as pit holes and field corners can make even more successful gamebird nest sites. Such places often produce a suitable balance of grass and herbaceous growth, which should also provide the correct conditions with undisturbed ground for benevolent insects. In addition these sites are often less vulnerable to predation because they are off the normal ground-vermin hunting routes.

Another technique to increase nesting cover is to deliberately lay tree tops and their trimmings in areas so that they help to hold up annual vegetation which might otherwise be flattened by heavy wind, rain, or even livestock. Fencing out of farm animals, and the planting of odd pockets of ground with native shrubs can go a long way to providing extra nesting cover. The more such suitable cover is available the greater the choice for gamebirds. Also it becomes increasingly difficult for predators to hunt out each individual nest.

Perhaps even more important on dairy farms and where silage and hay is made is the danger that a shortage of natural nesting cover may force birds to nest in the grass crops. Every year thousands of incubating hens are inavoidably mowed in

A low hedge will give shelter to a wood on flat ground. If deciduous, it should be regularly trimmed to an A-shape.

May and early June or engulfed by the forage harvester and converted into high protein animal feed. A similar holocaust can occur where grass and lucerne are grown for processing into stockfeed cubes. It is very difficult to dislodge an incubating gamebird from her nest. Dogging the fields is generally unsuccessful because the pheasants and partridges lose much of their scent during this stage as a natural defence mechanism against predation. The areas concerned are often very large and the pollen in such a crop tends to blunt the scenting powers even of gundogs. Special devices such as a flushing bar, a series of springy tines which precede the mower blades and physically force the birds off their nests do not work well with the density of forage crops currently grown. Also, modern grass cutting machinery tends to travel at speeds which make the tines inoperative.

In hay crops they can be partially effective because by late June the sward is sometimes a little thinner in the base. Also many of the hens have hatched their clutches and can lead their chicks away from the area. It may be helpful therefore, if cutting can start at the middle of the field, working outwards, or at least be taken in strips, leaving the outer two or three swarths standing overnight. This gives the brood a chance to draw out into the neighbouring fields and cover. In practice the pressures of modern farming and the urgency of completing agricultural operations at the optimum time mean that even these steps are only taken by the most enthusiastic shooting farmers. Therefore the most practical measure is to do everything possible to ensure sufficient suitable nesting sites in the hedgerows, field boundaries, odd corners and other uncultivated areas.

As a temporary solution a line of big bales will make an instant hedge around a draughty covert.

153

Lines of topped conifers produce a most effective windproof hedge.

Warming woodlands for game

To hold gamebirds, in particular pheasants, in woodland it is necessary to provide for their comfort. In harsh inclement weather they will normally seek out a sheltered site, while on a bright morning especially after a shower of rain they can frequently be found basking in the sun. Therefore the successful game covert should incorporate both of these features.

The pheasant lives most of the daylight hours on the ground so it is important to reduce the wind at this level. A low tight hedge will give shelter to a wood on flat ground. An evergreen hedge is ideal because it is during the winter months that protection from cold wind is needed most. *Lonicera nitida* is ideal in many respects. It grows quickly except in very exposed cold sites: plants can be grown from cuttings; it is not greatly favoured by rabbits, hares, or deer; and it requires relatively little management. Quickthorn is a more natural alternative but it must be laid or regularly trimmed to an 'A' shape if it is to afford any significant barrier to the wind. On sloping ground it will be necessary to provide shelter at different levels, and some lines or groups of evergreen shrubs or trees should be included at intervals to ensure this. Tree hedges such as those grown with cypress or spruce are excellent for shelter but they tend to produce an ugly picture frame effect around small woods and copses. This can be softened by mixing in other deciduous species or even planting a further row of low and medium height amenity trees as a screen for the evergreens. The second problem with tree hedges

Hedges should be planted several metres out from woods so that they have sufficient light to grow. The area between will be valuable as nesting cover and for machinery trimming the hedge.

154

Where farm and forest meet, the correct profile is important to avoid shading the field and to lead the wind over the wood.

is that the bottom branches tend to die off after a number of years, and it is at ground level that wind protection is most necessary for gamebirds. Die-back of the lower laterals can be reduced by topping young conifers at 2-3 m (6-10 ft) but it is often difficult to persuade a forester or farmer to take this action after he has spent years struggling to establish the plants.

Where farm and forest meet it is important to ensure the correct profile to the woodland edge. Particularly on the north side of a wood tall trees will cast shadows over the farm headland, and the tree roots will also travel out under the agricultural crop, competing with it for moisture and nutrients. To limit shading, it is preferable to plant coverts running in a north/south direction. This will also help the sun to penetrate into the centre of the woodland throughout the day, giving warmth, which is the second vital requirement to make it attractive for game.

There are two ways in which provision can be made to allow daylight into a wood. Obviously leaving an area unplanted will make an opening or ride but there are also certain tree species which have a sufficiently light canopy to permit some sunshine to permeate through to ground level. A high proportion of deciduous species is desirable inside the outer shelter zone. Larch, birch, cherry, and oak, are a few attractive trees which fit into this category. Oak are particularly valuable because they also produce acorns, much favoured by pheasants, but it is the ability to allow sufficient light to filter through their canopy for a shrub layer to survive on the ground that is the most important aspect of forest trees for game.

Sun must penetrate the tree canopy if shrub cover is to grow and survive.

Of the hardwoods, beech and sycamore are notorious for shading out ground cover, making woods too bare and draughty for game.

Some species are notoriously bad in that their leaves are too big and dense. The result is that few, if any, shrubs can survive below them. Probably the worst offenders in this respect are beech, sycamore, the maples and chestnut, of the hardwoods; and the firs, cypresses and spruces of the softwoods. A few groups of any of these within a wood can be accommodated and indeed small groups of the latter may provide valuable warm roosting. However, any large areas will ultimately turn into dark, draughty, compartments with little game-holding cover especially when the cold of the winter sets in.

Showing birds from and within woodland

The majority of shooting people are primarily interested in the opportunity to try their skill on sporting quarry. Therefore presentation of birds, particularly on a driven shoot, is vital to the success of a day. This begins with careful siting of coverts, correct positioning of guns, and controlled flushing at appropriate places.

Especially in woodland, a common fault is to allow pheasants to run to the end of the drive before they take wing. This may result in the bird, after peering gloomily at the guns, electing to 'go back'. Alternatvely, they may fly forward with insufficient time and distance to attain any great speed or height. Sewelling or flushing wire, discussed in the previous chapter, placed at a suitable distance back from the gunstand is often a successful means of avoiding both of these problems.

Livestock must be fenced out of game coverts! They can destroy ground cover in no time.

156

Fig.33a Aerial view of a flushing point. Note the D-shape of low ground cover, the gap for sewelling, the medium height rising area, and finally the tall forest trees.

It is astonishing how often no effort is made to take advantage of this simple technique.

The launching of pheasants can be critical not only to their height over the guns but also to their direction of flight. A bird that has forced its way up through a dense tree canopy is often exhausted when it finally reaches the top and may just glide down. Therefore a flushing point should provide for sufficient open spaces to form flight paths for pheasants to take off at a reasonable angle without impediment. Plenty of ground cover before the rising area is obviously vital, so that a gradual flush can be produced. Equally, too large or dense a growth of vegetation may result in difficulties for the beaters driving the birds.

Fig.33b The side view shows how birds are able to take off at an angle of about 30° with a clear line of flight.

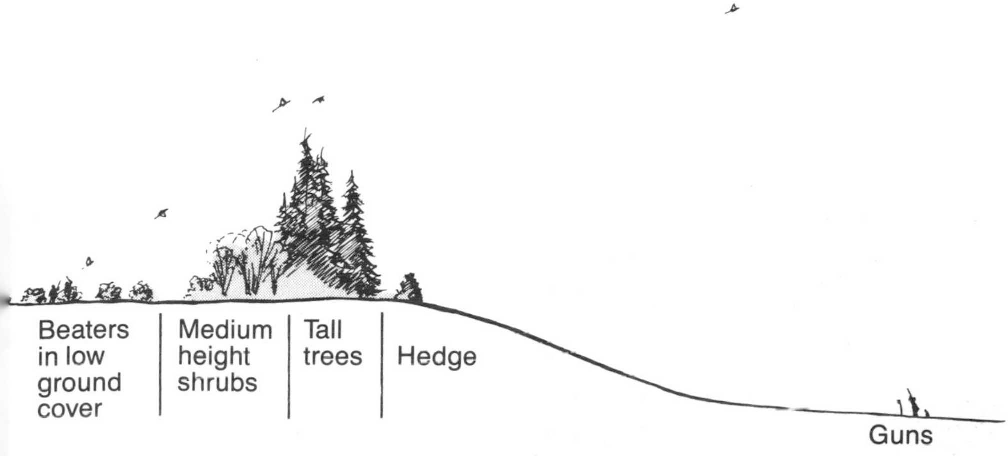

Beaters
in low
ground
cover

Medium
height
shrubs

Tall
trees

Hedge

Guns

(Left) Topping groups of spruce can make excellent warm sunny areas. The tops of Norway spruce can be sold as Christmas trees.

(Right) In large woods, rides may provide the only places where shooting is possible. If made in valley bottoms they make it easier to show high birds.

In theory the ideal flushing area should aim to provide a number of accessible collecting areas throughout the wood where birds will tuck in under cover. Clumps of low-growing shrubs such as bramble, snowberry, wild privet, *Lonicera*, raspberry, box, or topped spruce can all produce such cover. If well distributed this should produce a continual flow of birds over the guns throughout the drive. However, in bare woods, a proportion of birds are likely to run forward to the sewelling or flushing wire where shrub cover is particularly important. Beyond this an area of tall shrubs and medium height trees should make a suitable rising area. Species such as coppiced hazel, sweet chestnut, laurel, *Cotoneaster sps.* and heavily thinned or even topped deciduous trees are all excellent. Finally some tall timber before the gunstand should force pheasants at least to tree-top height provided the branches are not so sparse that it is easier for the birds to fly through.

With relatively small coverts sited at suitable distances apart, especially where guns are placed out in the open, pheasants may continue to rise after leaving the drive. However, in large woods of 5 hectares (12 acres) or more, it is often difficult to persuade birds to fly out of them. In this situation shooting across rides may be the only answer. It is obviously vital that guns have a chance to see the birds for sufficient time to swing onto them. In coniferous woodland at least a chain width is desirable. In deciduous trees it is sometimes possible to obtain a good enough view to shoot on narrower rides after leaf fall. In fact, some guns find they are more accurate when they have only a glimpse and a brief period in which to fire. However, if there is to be much hope of making the birds rise above the tops of the trees a wider ride of 45 m (50 yds) or more is required. This is so that pheasants actually have an opportunity to see the guns, which is the main method by which they may be persuaded to rise any higher.

Wide rides where commercial forestry is important do result in a reduction of croppable timber area, but normally a relatively small percentage of the total potential growing area is actually sacrificed. There are some possible advantages. Wide rides make good firebreaks, and they offer access routes for the foresters and their machinery when operations such as thinning, brashing, and even harvesting are undertaken. For game and wildlife there is a host of benefits. There will be more edge, so important in governing the available territories for pheasants. There will be further sunny areas for warmth and drying out after rain. In addition such rides can be extremely valuable for deer both in providing feed/grazing and a suitable area for their control. Lastly, well maintained rides often greatly enhance the amenity value of woodlands, making it possible to actually see some of their most attractive features.

Developing derelict woods

Throughout Great Britain there are hectares of old woodland which have become too bare, draughty and cold to hold game. Some areas are devoid of ground cover because commercial forestry management dictates a selection of tree species that allow insufficient light through to the floor of the wood for shrub growth to survive. But there are thousands of acres of copses, spinneys, belts and larger woodland which are unsuitable for game mainly because of a lack of management.

Traditional mixed hardwoods which might comprise forest trees such as oak, ash, and sometimes some beech, hornbeam, sycamore, cherry, or sweet chestnut often have an understorey of coppice. Hazel coppice is predominant in the south of England, but in Kent and Sussex there are also large areas of hornbeam coppice, once used for making fine quality charcoal, a constituent of the traditional blackpowder. Sadly, the demand for hornbeam for charcoal and for hazel for hurdle-making or thatching spiles has diminished. Sweet chestnut, which is so favoured for making fencing materials is possibly the main coppice crop that still has particular value, other than for firewood.

The value to game of these woods, where no use can be found for the coppice, is limited. Cutting areas and allowing fresh growth from the stool provides only a temporary answer. Unless demand for hazel suddenly re-appears the same situation is likely to arise through regrowth in a decade or so. In some parts, particularly those close to a high population, there is scope for coppicing of certain species like ash, sycamore, and hornbeam as a firewood crop. The advent of the wood-burning stove increased the demand for wood fuel and now that much of the sad remains of Dutch Elm disease has been consumed the owners of these burners are having to look elsewhere to feed them.

Woodland that is coppiced on a regular rotation with small areas cut each year often provides near perfect game-holding habitat. It is the mixed age structure that provides birds with 'meat and two veg'. Some open, sunny areas, other parts with good ground vegetation for shelter and escape cover, and some bare areas for shade, foraging and easy movement under the heavier canopy of a section soon to require cutting again makes ideal pheasant holding habitat. This sort of woodland can also prove popular in the winter for woodcock.

However, where there is no likelihood of coppicing being practised for commercial reasons in the foreseeable future it is up to the shoot to try and let some light onto the forest floor. Some care needs to be taken in this operation. Large clearances are likely to produce too big an area of shrub regrowth when the ground vegetation does recover. Bearing in mind that it is always easier to cut a little more later than to replace cut trees, circles of about 10 to 15 m (33-50 ft) diameter might be suitable in the first instance. These should be spread at intervals throughout the covert, the aim being to produce manageable clumps of well-distributed cover and shelter.

Any poles above 10 cm (4 in.) diameter may be worth stacking in cords for firewood. However, tops and side branches if carefully stacked in lines in the direction of the drive will be of value in forming temporary cover. In addition they will provide a framework for brambles to climb and will help hold nettles and annual vegetation upright after early autumn frosts.

In areas where there is limited demand for firewood it may pay to kill the regrowth from the coppiced stump by spraying it the following season. Also, for the longer term, attempts can be made to restock the woodland with suitable forest species. Thanks to the recent invention of simple individual guards such as tree-shelters which will protect young transplants against rabbits, hares and deer, it is possible to establish groups of hardwoods without surrounding the area in rabbit netting or deer fencing. If some groups of softwoods are considered to be of greater value, then bio-degradable plastic netting guards can be used. The large-mesh sizes allow the lateral branches to spread. For game, this is most important for providing both shelter and cover in the early stages.

Each year the Game Conservancy advisory service are called in to help over the siting, planning, and planting of hundreds of acres of new spinneys, copses, belts and small woods. Thousands of acres of existing woodland are visited to see how best they can be improved, restocked, and developed for shooting. This is a mere fraction of the afforested areas that are preserved, managed, and maintained because of the sporting interests of farmers, landowners, and others. For many quarry species woodland is the prime habitat. If there is sufficient suitable warmth and shelter for game in the woods there will be less need to sacrifice agricultural ground and invest in areas of special food or cover crop.

14 Thanksgiving, Clearing-up and Reviewing Results

Gratuities

On every shoot there is a great tribe of people who in some way contribute to the success of the season. Often this is purely because of their interest and natural enthusiasm. It may be the man at the lodge gate who keeps an eye out for strange cars and records the numbers, the neighbouring forester who has donated some offcuts for the construction of tunnels during the trapping season, or the spinster who gives permission to pick up in her garden. For all who help, a brace of pheasants, perhaps a bottle of whisky or something similar, depending on the recipient, can go such a long way to ensuring continued goodwill and assistance. Thanks giving to those who contribute out of kindness is particularly important in current conditions when not everyone is in wholehearted support of traditional country sports.

Keeper's day and cocks only

For those with a more deep-seated interest in game management and shooting such as beaters and pickers up, it pays handsome dividends to repay these favours with an end of season shoot for those who enjoy their sport.

On one shoot near Fordingbridge the system goes a stage further. Instead of any cash payment, the beaters are given two days to try their skills. One is usually a cocks only but the other may be a 'formal' partridge day. The result is that the beaters are all particularly keen. In this case the other benefit is that the regular guns beat for the day and derive considerable amusement at watching the beaters outclassed by some driven birds. At the same time they learn about some of the problems of presenting sporting game.

It can be an advantage to plan and hold the 'beaters and helpers' day before the very end of the season. Although absolutely deadly at pigeons over decoys or bolted rabbits, sometimes they are not the most accurate of shots at driven birds! Consequently, if the day is also to be a serious attempt at thinning out the cock pheasant stocks in addition to entertaining the beaters then the operation may fail to meet either objective. Cocks only shoots towards the end of the season are common in areas of reasonable wild pheasant production, but because birds tend to fly particularly well at the end of the season, some prefer to allow only 'high' hens for several days instead of cocks only on the last few shoots.

Another successful system for rationing the number of hens shot is to allow guns to shoot them only after a certain number have been seen flushing from individual drives. One person needs to do the counting and should give a clear sign, such as a blast on a whistle, when hens may be shot during the drive. On some pheasant shoots the first day or two of the season is restricted to cocks only. This can be a useful method of limiting the bag at a period when there are plenty of birds in the coverts and it may also help to cull some of the wily old campaigners.

Frequently the opportunity to try new drives or to beat coverts in different directions is taken on the helpers day. The results can be totally misleading for a number of reasons. Towards the end of the season the birds are probably at their wildest and therefore likely to run furiously as soon as the first shots of the day are fired. Of course, with many of the beating team armed, this tends to be the one day in the season when stops are forgotten or at least not taken sufficiently seriously. Also for the same reason, the beating itself is liable to be sub-standard. At this time of year a false impression can be gained as to the birds' flying ability, which is likely to be much greater at the end of January than earlier in the season. However, this does not mean that reversing the occasional drive or leaving a generous number of back guns is not an excellent way of outwitting a number of wily old cocks who might be better in the bag than remaining on the shoot for the following breeding season.

The most important aspect of the end of season beaters and helpers day is that there may be a number of guns who may not shoot regularly in company. It is therefore absolutely vital that safety is taken especially seriously. Clear instructions as to what may be shot must be issued. If dogs, particularly terriers, are in use, then it is sometimes wise to ban the shooting of ground game. If both standing guns and some 'walkers' are armed then the latter should only be allowed to shoot at game going back. There is seldom much skill or pleasure involved in shooting a pheasant which is rising out of cover compared to a driven bird. An even safer alternative is to place standing back guns in a suitable place behind the beating line.

For those shoots where for some reason it is difficult to organise special days for the beaters and helpers a chance to go pigeon roost shooting or decoying on crops after the game season will probably be greatly appreciated. Even lamping rabbits at night may provide the spur to encourage real enthusiasm into the team.

Equipment – hygiene and storage

Even for the thoroughly experienced professional headkeeper the word disease can instigate a feeling of worry and unease, if not panic. Here is one aspect of game management where knowledge is never complete and where risks cannot totally be avoided but have somehow to be minimised.

Hygiene still hinges mainly on basic cleanliness achieved primarily by scrubbing!

The Game Conservancy's special Gamekeepers' Refresher Course concentrates heavily on gamebird diseases for this very reason. Every pathologist stresses that old dictum 'prevention is better than cure'. One can also go a stage further by saying that on the rearing field there are a host of disinfectants, cures and chemicals for all sorts of situation, but that there is no substitute in basic hygiene for old-fashioned cleanliness, achieved primarily by heavy scrubbing with the use of much elbow grease.

All rules have exceptions and strangely enough there are diseases where total prevention may not be better than cure. Coccidiosis is one of these where a minor infection should lead to the build-up of a natural immunity in the flock. Therefore a brief dose of disease followed by a quick cure in the controlled conditions of the rearing field can be preferable to a violent outbreak in release pens or the wild state where treatment with the appropriate drugs is often difficult, if not impossible.

However, thorough cleansing and treatment of equipment is, together with a care not to overcrowd, a sound recipe for keeping disease disasters at a distance. Gamekeepers frequently ask which is the best chemical to use for cleansing game equipment. It is wise to choose a product which has been extensively used as a poultry disinfectant, and 'Ministry approved' unless a particular disease has been identified when a specific compound targeted at that ailment may be available. In this case coccidiosis provides a useful example in that many disinfectants do little to the tough encysted spores of this disease. In fact a 1% solution of ammonia or solutions that produce ammonia, applied with considerable care, is the recommended method of treating pens and equipment where an outbreak of this all too prevalent protozoa has occurred.

In addition to soaking, scrubbing and treating kit before stowing away for the winter, it is a sound precaution to check for defects, wear and tear, and if dealing with wooden articles, give a coat of preservative such as creosote, unless the timber has been previously impregnated with tannin. It can be particularly dangerous to creosote the inside of brooder houses just before the rearing season when the heat from the brooder can drive off fumes which may prove toxic to the chicks. Sections, and all wood items, should be stacked off the ground to prevent moisture permeating into the pores and accelerating rot. Roof nets are particularly susceptible to gnawing by rats and mice and should be hung from a wire or string in bundles so as to be safe from these rodent pests. Plastics can also deteriorate rapidly in ultra-violet light, so they should be stored in a dark-coloured sack or bag.

Frequently, shooting people enquire about the availability of an efficient treatment for the ground which will kill off dormant disease spores. Sadly there is no totally effective soil sterilant that is practical but some consider a solution of Jeyes fluid or other compounds of value, while the old 'keeper's idea of liming the ground is based on sound scientific evidence. Gapes, one of the most prevalent gamebird diseases, has a stage of its life cycle which involves invertebrates, particularly slugs, worms and snails, as an alternative host (as mentioned in

Chapter 8). In general these creatures thrive in neutral soil conditions. Therefore liming, which increases the pH, should reduce them on alkali soils. However, care must be taken, for in acid areas liming will neutralise the ground and improve the conditions for these alternate hosts and therefore the chances of the gapeworm overwintering in them.

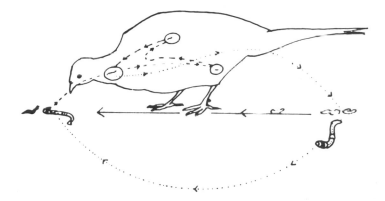

Fig.35 The gapeworm, which can infect the windpipe of gamebirds, causing one of the most common gamebird diseases, can be carried by invertebrates such as snails, slugs and earthworms as alternative hosts. An effective treatment of the ground involves understanding this life cycle.

Winter is often the only time to check and service equipment that may require repair. Brooder heaters, and houses, nursery pens, sections, automatic drinkers, calor gas automatic change-over valves are but a few of the items which may require overhaul. The next season will arrive soon enough, and it pays to be as prepared as possible in a business which is plagued by all too many natural imponderables.

Reviewing the results

Long before the last shot of one year or season has been fired, thoughts will have turned to the next. Certain decisions may already have had to be taken. As mentioned, special game crop areas often have to be decided eighteen months in advance in sites where the agricultural system involves winter cereals. By February 1st it will be too late to ask for a selected strip to be drilled for birds if the field concerned is already under autumn sown corn. Suggesting to a farmer that he might consider ploughing in a strip of growing crop is either going to produce some 'flowery' language or be very expensive in terms of compensation.

Where wild game can produce a sufficient surplus to provide shooting each season without the requirement to rear, the most critical decision may be how much stock should be left. Over a period of years an idea will emerge as to the numbers of partridges, pheasant, and even duck, to aim to leave as the spring stock. It largely depends on the availability of suitable habitat and territory size which can only be established by experience of the individual place. For partridges the results of spring pair counts in March will give a good indication of the number of territories on a particular shoot. At least enough birds should be left to fill all these together with a generous margin over to allow for winter loss.

Pheasants, of course, are different in that only the cock is territorial and he is polygamous while the ladies are promiscuous. Travelling through parts of East Anglia in the spring it astonishes many to see what huge stocks of hen birds are deliberately left on the ground. Where the habitat and farming system are sympathetic the results after a warm dry spring and early summer can be spectacular. Of course, with no catching up, incubation, rearing or releasing, the 'keeper can devote his entire time and energy to vigorous predator control and caring for his wild stock.

For those who have to rely to an extent on the game farm or the rearing field to supplement their wild population the plans for the forthcoming year may be simpler to make. Much will depend on the information available from the results of previous seasons. In particular, wing tag returns can play a revolutionary part in improving results by revealing futile and wasted expense of past plans.

If tags have been applied then the total number of wild and immigrant birds will be known. Where, by good fortune, neighbouring shoots tag then an even more accurate figure for wild production can be established. If, after a number of seasons, this proves to be an insignificant figure then a deliberate decision not to leave such a stock can be taken. However, during the fifty years of Game Conservancy research and advisory work it is staggering how often the opposite situation has been proved by tagging experiments. Shoots which had been releasing 500 poults annually and shooting 400 with reasonable regularity quite falsely assumed that most of these were their own restocked birds. So often they discovered by marking that they were actually shooting only 100 of the released pheasants, a miserable 20%, not the highly unlikely 80% they were so confident about. With this information it should be a simple matter to improve results by releasing less and devoting more care, attention, and time to the truly wild stock. In fact, the Game Conservancy National Game Census, which collects facts and figures from over one million acres of shooting, shows that the average recovery rate for reared pheasants on well managed ground is now around the 40% mark.

What happens to the remainder, apart from what are left as breeding stock, is a matter of considerable importance. Research so far suggests that a proportion, often 20%, never survive release. Investigations by advisory staff on individual shoots frequently find that the quality of pens and attention to gradual acclimatisation to the wild is the key to successful restocking.

If a number of release pens are employed in an area, whether for partridges or pheasants, invaluable information can be revealed if coloured and/or numbered

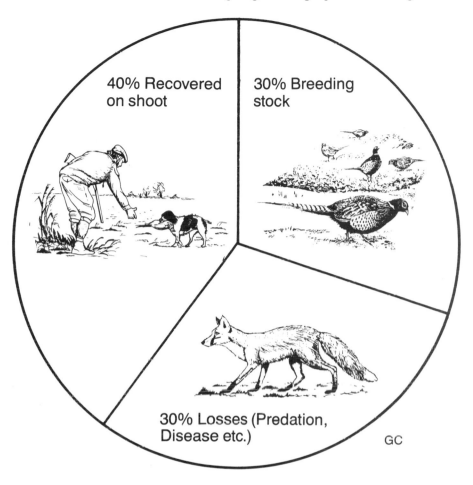

40% Recovered on shoot

30% Breeding stock

30% Losses (Predation, Disease etc.)

GC

Fig.36 Fate of reared pheasants (tagged) in the first year after release. (Figures from Game Conservancy National Game Census).

tags are used. Obviously if certain release sites give consistently poor returns, it is a simple matter to drop them in favour of more successful positions. This can only be realised if the birds have been marked and the returned tags are carefully recorded as described in Chapter 8. Indeed, further information on drift and the directions in which birds are inclined to stray will also show up if the tags are collected or recorded by the individual drive.

For the real enthusiast who has collected the tags from birds shot, whether partridges or pheasants, by the drive and recorded these results a picture of which release areas feed the various drives can be drawn. Ultimately it is exciting sport with high, fast, twisting, or turning targets that exhilarate the shooter. Once the real classic drives are known, if one is also aware of which pens fed them then by

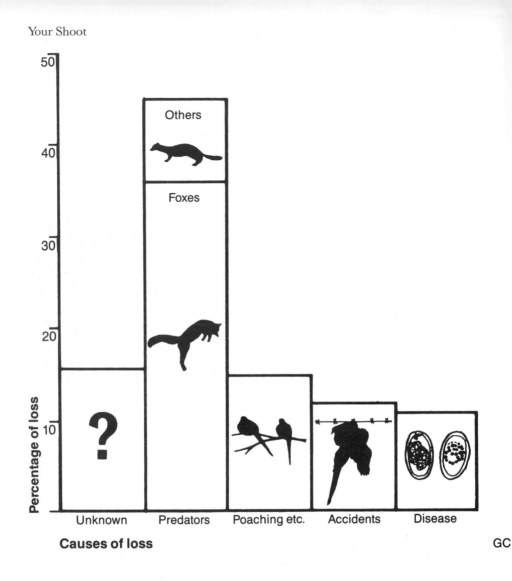

Fig.37 Causes of losses of reared pheasants after release.

diverting more of next season's release to these there should be a good chance of them providing quantity as well as quality. However, when making plans for the future on the evidence of the past it pays to be cautious, especially if there is only one year's findings and results available. Thank the Lord that every season is different because it is the uncertainty and chance that makes shooting and all field sports the fascinating pastimes that they are.

To improve anything generally involves increasing expenditure of money or time. Beware of building up so big an operation that the costs suddenly loom so large that some of the team or syndicate can no longer afford to participate.

(Above) A country landscape dominated by food production.

(Below) A country landscape where an interest in shooting and field sports has resulted in game and wildlife habitat not only being conserved but also created.

Good game management and effective 'keepering are all part and parcel of producing enjoyable, exciting, and varied days of shooting, while caring for the countryside and conserving and cropping a wildlife population. There is always a strong element of chance and luck, but with greater knowledge there should be greater opportunity to ensure the future of game and wildlife in a constantly changing environment. Thirteen thousand sportsmen care enough to support the Game Conservancy and ensure future research into the survival of game.

The results of these scientific studies are then translated into new practical techniques which, together with more than fifty years of game management experience, are available to all through the Game Conservancy Advisory Service. On-the-spot advice, a wide variety of special courses, and a series of practical booklets cater in different ways for those who enjoy shooting, 'keeper ground, manage a shoot, or just enjoy seeing game and a countryside which will support it.

Books for Further Reading

Game Conservancy Advisory Booklets

No. Title

2 *Game and Shooting Crops* – details of crops for game cover and feed.

3 *Wildfowl Management on Inland Waters* – flight ponds, hatching, rearing, releasing, wild duck breeding areas.

5 *Egg Production and Incubation* – Basic planning re-stocking, catching up, laying pens and their management, feeding.

6 *Diseases of Gamebirds and Wildfowl* – includes illustrations in colour, drugs and vaccines, notes on cleaning and disinfecting.

7 *Farm Hazards to Game and Wildlife.*

8 *Pheasant Rearing and Releasing* – including open field and brooder rearing, feeding, releasing and acclimatising to the wild.

9 *Game Records* – deals with the grey and red-legged partridges, pheasant, grouse and mallard.

12 *Grouse Management* – covers the techniques applied to both the management of birds and the heather.

14 *Feeding and Management of Game in Winter* – hand, hopper and automatic feeding, dusting shelters and feed staddles, watering in covert.

15 *Woodlands for Pheasants* – planning a new wood, layouts of coverts, shelter belts, spinneys, woodlands, forestry operations, shrubs.

16 *Predator and Squirrel Control* – discusses species which may be controlled, methods, and the current legal situation.

17 *Roe Deer* – Management and Stalking – with a special section on mortality and disease.

18 *Red-legged Partridges* – some notes on their biology, management, rearing and releasing.

21 *The European Woodcock* – a search of the literature since 1940 by Monica Shorten.

22 *Rabbit Control* – methods of control

or *The Complete Book of Game Conservation* – a compendium of the above.

Other Books

The Amateur Keeper – Archie Coats (published by Andre Deutsch)
The D.I.Y. Game Shoot – John Humphreys (published by David and Charles)

The Game Conservancy

The Game Conservancy is an independent research, information and advisory organisation funded primarily by membership subscription. It originated in 1933 when ICI's Eley Cartridge Division initiated a research programme to identify the causes of a decline of wild partridges. In 1946 they acquired Burgate Manor, Fordingbridge as an HQ and a nearby farm on which to study game and develop management and 'keepering techniques appropriate for the changed post-war conditions. By 1969 the Eley Game Advisory Station had grown so large that the hitherto free service had to be withdrawn, and after a merger with The Game Research Association, a new organisation The Game Conservancy was formed to continue and expand this research and advisory work but funded by public subscription, sponsorship and fee-paying services.

The Game Conservancy's research team of twelve scientists is currently investigating pheasant management, wild partridge production, cereal growing and gamebirds, the development of new areas of inland waters for wildfowl, grouse in the north of England and Scotland, the diseases of game, and the effects and importance of predation on game and wildlife. Studies, some specially funded, have recently been completed on the redlegged partridge, hedgerows for game nesting, the roe deer, the brown hare and the woodcock. The results of research are applied to developing practical management techniques. Information is made available through membership publications, advisory booklets, specialist courses, and through the team of experienced game advisers. Our longest serving consultant has calculated that, since the war, he has been involved in the planting of 11,000 acres of new woodland for game and the management and replanting of 198,000 acres. The contribution this must have made to wildlife conservation and the enhancement of the landscape needs no emphasis.

The objectives of the Game Conservancy are to conduct research into the future of game in the countryside and to provide information and advice for practical application. By providing scientific facts and objective advice the Game Conservancy works with other organisations to influence the formulation of legislation, whether in the context of shooting or wildlife and game populations, both in the UK and in Brussels.

It has been said that if only the corncrake flew like a pheasant or tasted like a partridge it would not now be such a very rare bird!

Richard Van Oss
Director, The Game Conservancy

173

The Game Conservancy Advisory Service
can help to improve your shoot

GC

The Game Conservancy has always found that giving practical advice on the ground is the most effective way to help farmers, landowners, shoot managers and gamekeepers.

Experienced consultants cover the whole of the British Isles and aim to assist sportsmen to improve the quality of their shooting through sound management.

Suggestions often involve improvements to the habitat, particularly in woodlands, where they are least likely to conflict with the farm or estate. Advice is given on the design, siting and planting of hundreds of acres of small woodlands and coverts for game, wildlife and amenity each year.

Special game crops, pest and predator control, rearing and releasing techniques, winter management and feeding, the presentation of sporting birds, grouse and moorland management, wildfowl, woodland deer, assessing shooting potential and shoot costs, are the main subjects on which shoots most frequently request advice.

With the increasing costs of producing shooting, the modest fee for a full or half-day visit by an adviser is usually repaid in a very short time from improved results.

Game Management and 'Keepers Training Courses

A wide range of both residential and one-day courses are held each year to cater for the needs of gamekeepers, professional and amateur, farmers, land managers and shooting men. All of the courses are described in detail on a special leaflet produced early each year. They are based on a blend of illustrated lectures and outdoor demonstrations with practical participation by those attending wherever possible.

The range includes:

Residential	Length of Course in Days
Gamekeepers' Training Course	8
Experienced 'Keepers Refresher Course	2½
Young Shots Courses	3
Part-time 'Keepers Course	2½

Regional

A series of Game Management Days and one-day Part-time 'Keepers' Courses. These are held at different venues throughout Great Britain each year.

For a Course Leaflet or further details of the Advisory Service, please contact The Advisory Department, The Game Conservancy, Fordingbridge, Hants SP6 1EF. Tel: Fordingbridge (0425) 52381.

GC

The British Association for Shooting and Conservation (B.A.S.C.)

The British Association for Shooting and Conservation was founded in 1908 as the Wildfowlers' Association of Great Britain and Ireland (WAGBI). Today, with a membership in excess of 65,000, it represents the interests of all who shoot live quarry, seeking to promote the highest standards of safety, sportsmanship and courtesy among the shooting public, and to foster a practical interest in, and contribution to wildlife management, and the conservation of the countryside upon which shooting depends.

Recognising that the future of shooting depends upon both the quarry and its habitat, the B.A.S.C. works closely with local, national and international sporting and conservation bodies to ensure that shooting retains its important place within the management of sensitive and scientifically important habitats. Meanwhile, the Association maintains strong political representation locally, at Westminster, and at European level.

Through an active education programme, the Association promotes basic levels of proficiency and sportsmanship in the shooting field. It runs a wide range of courses and training schemes, publishes educational literature, and gives information and advice to members on matters related to sporting shooting.

The B.A.S.C. endeavours to ensure that the sportsman's voice is heard, wherever and whenever decisions are made which affect the future of our sport, and it seeks the support of all those who shoot. Further details can be obtained from The British Association for Shooting and Conservation, Marford Mill, Rossett, Wrexham, Clwyd LL12 0HL. Tel: Rossett (0244) 570881.

Index